I0814711

WHAT PEOPLE ARE SAYING ABOUT *FEARLESS*

Fearless, Tracey Mitchell's beautifully written new book will equip and empower you to pick up a slingshot and defeat your personal giants—then go skydiving.

—Ron Hall
Author, #1 NYT Bestseller
Same Kind of Different as Me

In some way, we all face the giant of fear. If you are looking for inspiration or encouragement, Tracey Mitchell has captured both in her new book *Fearless*.

Tracey's message is clear, "Face your fears but don't get stuck in them. . . ."

—Anne Beiler
Founder of Auntie Anne's pretzels
Author and Speaker

Sometimes our mindset is the only thing that stands between us and our greatest breakthrough. Honest. Vulnerable. Thought-provoking. Tracey Mitchell's new book is a call to courage. *Fearless* is not a shallow read but a revelation of what our lives and the world can look like if we ditch our doubts and take bold, daring leaps of faith. A forward thinker, Tracey Mitchell blends captivating stories with profound truths to give us a taste of what Fearless living embodies. She emphasizes that if we are to live out our purpose, "It's time we shatter messages that morph our faith and shatter our courage."

—Alita Reynolds
President, Women of Faith

Plainly . . . *Fearless* will make you uncomfortable with mediocre living. Fiery and passionate Tracey Mitchell challenges you to rise above your fears and chase after your dreams. If you want to enlarge your life, dive into this book. You will never look at life the same way again, and you will be in a position to "Conquer the Beast "in your life.

—Scott Mendes
World Champion Bull Rider
Hall of Fame Bull Rider

We're in a window of time caused by the Covid pandemic when people are choosing to change direction with their lives and careers. With ongoing uncertainties, disruptions, and fear, many have regrettably chosen isolation, depression, and loneliness. But Tracey Mitchell's book F*earless: Wildly Optimistic in a Worry-Filled World* will embolden you to be fiercely bullish and choose a life of fearless joy.

— Kathleen Cooke
Co-Founder of Cooke Media Group
and The Influence Lab
Author of *Hope 4 Today: Stay Connected to God in a Distracted Culture*

Tracey Mitchell is one of the greatest wordsmiths of the 21st century. As a friend of many years, I can assure you that she demonstrates fearless living. I've watched her speak to thousands and have witnessed her words transform the lives of others—moving them from a place of mediocrity to maximized living.

In her latest work, *Fearless,* she offers insights and revelation on how to eradicate the strongholds of anxiety, doubt, and apprehension. She uses biblical application, contemporary analogies, and personal stories to empower the reader to rise above the chaos of the culture. *Fearless* is a must-read for pastors, business owners, and visionaries.

—Bishop James Payne
President, JPM, Inc.

Essential. Necessary. Transformative. Tracey Mitchell is passionate about empowering this generation to cast off the ropes of conformity and run headlong into freedom. In *Fearless*, Tracey vividly describes the rewards and benefits of being wildly optimistic in a worry-filled word. This work is full of transformative truths and yet, deeply personal. *Fearless* is a fresh word for a world starved for passion, courage, and peace.

—Jenn Gotzon
Award-winning Actress, Producer, Speaker

Fearless is a timely message to our present generation. Tracey Mitchell's words will challenge you to live life without excuses. Regardless of how helpless or hopeless your situation may seem, this book will inspire you to believe that your best days are just ahead.

—Dr. Tracy Strawberry
Author of Individual and Family Restoration Publications

Fearless: Wildly Optimistic in a Worry-Filled World. What a title! What a Goal! What a lifestyle! Tracey Mitchell lives fearlessly, and in her latest book, she passes on that courage by showing readers how they can be set free from the grip of worry and transform into warriors.

This book does not contain ethereal or abstract meanderings but achieves its purpose by applying dynamic, eternal principles that are relevant and functional to daily opportunities and challenges. It will move you from a position of fear to a place of success and influence.

—Dr. Mike Brown
ThD, Founder and President of Strength and Wisdom Ministries
Lead Pastor, Faith and Wisdom Church

Tracey Mitchell is one of the finest Bible teachers I know. Because of her in-depth study and mastery of Scripture, she always delights and fascinates us with surprising insights and her special way of grasping spiritual truths. Her writing is filled with turn-of-phrase descriptions that capture our imaginations and stir us to deeper understanding and service. Once again, as in her previous books, she does not disappoint us in *Fearless: Wildly Optimistic in a Worry-Filled World*. So do yourself a favor and dive into this challenging and refreshing experience. You'll be so glad you did.

—Mary Hollingsworth
Best-Selling Author and Publisher
Creative Enterprises Studio

Tracey Mitchell is a champion of success! I have known Tracey as a leader, motivator, gifted communicator, mentor to many, and best of all, as my friend. God has used her life to inspire thousands of people to live up to their God-given potential. This book will not only challenge your thinking, but it will also strengthen your faith that with God, nothing is impossible!

—Darrell Yarbrough
Lead Pastor, The Assembly at Warner Robins

Tracey Mitchell offers wisdom and real-life experiences to those on a quest for spiritual insight. Having worked with Tracey for more than a decade, one of the things I admire is her tenacious drive to lift others to greater heights. She is authentic and lives out the words that she communicates to others. As a paster, her transparency and integrity are traits that I want the members of our church to exemplify. Whether in conferences, churches, or various forms of media, Tracey delivers solid answers to complex issues. Fearless is an overflow of her courageous life; it will inspire you to live your faith out loud and without reservation.

—Asa Dockery
Senior Pastor, World Harvest Church North

In *Fearless: Wildly Optimistic in a Worry-Filled World,* Tracey Mitchell uncages courage. Artfully and compellingly, she reveals how crisis moments can catalyze change.

F*earless* isn't a soft or anesthetic read. This book is an invitation to go beyond the borders of what is comfortable and convenient—to seek purpose and live in expectation. For more than two decades, I have watched Tracey Mitchell live out the principles of this manuscript. I encourage you to follow in her footsteps and let your faith run wild.

—Sullen Roberts
Founder and Chairman, Christian Women in Media

Courage. Guts. Moxie. Describe an elite group of people who daringly exchange comfort and conformity for risk and reward. In *Fearless*, Tracey Mitchell pulls the reader out of their passivity and invites them to make a faith quest. Each section is artfully designed to move the reader forward in their faith, encouraging them to live beyond the borders of doubt, fear, or failure. This *fearless movement* is perfect for conferences, leadership training, or group study.

—Donnie Mooney
Senior Pastor, Life Church

A clarion call for courage! Tracey has a gift for speaking life-giving encouragement with thought-provoking calls to action. *Fearless: Wildly Optimistic in a Worry-Filled World* will give you confidence, wisdom, and motivation to walk in faith boldly.

—Misty Phillip
Founder of Spark Media
Award-winning author of *The Struggle is Real: But so is God* Bible Study

Dr. Tracey Mitchell is an authentic leader; her teachings and literary works reflect this integrity, and Fearless is no exception. In every one of her books, she addresses the deep emotions each of us faces—and her understanding of the scriptures reveals the heart of God toward us.

Fearless is a must-read for those who long to cast off fear and experience audacious faith. Let this book launch you forward, live without compromise, and never look back.

—Pastor Yvon Stabili
Assistant General Secretary IAOGI Canada

If you care deeply about pursuing long-term peace, put this book on your required reading list. Tracey Mitchell has assembled a brilliant 30-day experience that will challenge you to live outside of worry. Her gift of communication will invite you to practice a newfound hunger for living a life of optimism through Christ Jesus.

—Kenny Meckfessel
Lead Pastor, The Ridge

A wise man once said, "Never doubt in darkness what God spoke in the light." Fear can be crippling to your destiny, but God has called us to be fearless and courageous in the face of the enemy's devices. Tracey Mitchell's *Fearless* is a must-read for any individual desiring to bravely walk out the call of God on their life with the assurance that God is not only present but molding them in the process.

—Pastors Josh and Jennifer Palmer
Destiny Pointe Church

Fear is a growing epidemic causing tremendous despair on a global scale. It is the root cause of most anxieties, animosities, and relational fractures. Dr. Tracey Mitchell's book, *Fearless*, will equip you to face and conquer the tormenting issues that are minimizing your greatest potential and robbing you of abundant joy!

—Brenda Crouch
Author, Speaker, TV Host

The writing of Tracey Mitchell is on a level of excellence rarely seen in today's market. Her ability to paint a vivid picture with words is a powerful gift. However, that ability remains secondary to her commitment to the integrity of the Bible and her passion for revealing and celebrating the truths of God's anointed Word. Regardless of where a person is on their spiritual journey, her message will set them free from any pain of the past and propel them into greater Kingdom influence.

—Pastor Timothy Coats
Lead Pastor, Family First Church

Fearless is packed with salient solutions that will empower you to gain control of your life, destiny, and purpose while propelling you toward an intimate walk with the King of the universe. Tracey Mitchell carves out a prophetic path of progress for even the timidest believer. *Fearless* will help readers discover new fire, a renewed focus, and tackle the most challenging obstacles or opportunities.

—Dr. Chris Foster
Lead Pastor, City Church

In a world filled with chaos, disorder, and uncertainty, Tracey Mitchell unearths hope and confidence. Her unique communication style inspires readers to be tenacious, resilient, and faith-filled.

Fearless: Wildly Optimistic in a Worry-Filled World is a must-read for those who, as Tracey describes, "are daring enough to believe for the incredible and contend for the impossible." As a pastor and leader, I know this book will empower you to rise above the clamor of the culture so you can see things from a heavenly perspective.

—Pastor Glen Dorsey
Author and International Speaker

Tracey Mitchell is a very gifted author and communicator. In a worry-filled world, she is a voice of hope. Tracey's words will inspire you to live from a place of faith and not fear.

—David Overstreet
Lead pastor, Whitney Lane FWC

Few understand what it takes to be a brave, authentic leader in today's culture. As pastors, we know the importance of connecting with visionaries willing to rise above the tide of culture and risk reaching into people's pain. Dr. Tracey Mitchell provides answers and solutions for all generations, empowering others to walk in their God-ordained destiny.

Fearless: Wildly Optimistic in a Worry-Filled World is more than a book; it is a movement. It is perfect for leadership training, small groups, and Bible studies.

—Mike & Kristy Thomas
Lead Pastors, ROLC (River of Life Church)

Trouble finding the gold in the experiences of life? Dr. Tracey Mitchell gives perspective into many of the challenges we face by sharing 'fearless' thoughts. Take the time to let words sink deep, reflect, inspect, review, and mine the gold.

—David Steunenberg
Lead Pastor, Solid Rock Church

By equipping the reader with a literary magnifying glass, Tracey Mitchell gives an endoscopic look into the hidden issues of the heart. *Fearless* encourages the reader to assess the condition of their faith and develop strategies for spiritual growth. This book will "tether you to the truth" so you can launch into the future.

—Mike and Alicia Mason
Lead Pastors, The Assembly Hot Springs

Tracey Mitchell has a heart that is open to hearing the voice of the Holy Spirit. Her writing style is uniquely compelling, allowing her readers to experience scripture from a fresh perspective. *Fearless* is a must-read for leaders, visionaries, and dreamers.

—Terry and Cheryl Davis
Lead Pastors, Grace Community Church

You need this book! In *Fearless: Wildly Optimistic in a Worry-Filled World*, Tracey Mitchell reveals how the enemy of your soul schemes against the prophecies made over your future. Each chapter is insightful, infused with wisdom, and offers strategies to help you bypass any traps that would pull you away from your calling. Watch the enemy's plans collapse and crumble when you lean into God's promises.

—Kelly Parrish,
Conference Host and Women's Pastor

OTHER BOOKS WRITTEN BY TRACEY MITCHELL

Becoming Brave: How to Think Big, Dream Wildly, and Live Fear Free

The Invitation: to Intimacy with God

Downside Up: Transform Rejection into Your Golden Opportunity

FEARLESS

WILDLY OPTIMISTIC IN A Worry-Filled World

TRACEY MITCHELL

FOUR

Published by Four Rivers Media

Cover design by: Sara Young
Cover Photo by: David Porcheddu

ISBN: 978-1-957369-80-8 1 2 3 4 5 6 7 8 9 10

Printed in the United States of America

To the fearless ones who change the world.

Contents

SUDDENLY

"Behold, I am going to do something new, Now it will spring up; Will you not be aware of it? I will even make a roadway in the wilderness, Rivers in the desert."
—*Isaiah 43:19 (NASB)*

David grabbed his sword and tucked a dagger into his bag. He hunted venison, and mountain lions hunted him. The days were long, and at night, he slept in the fortress where runaways and renegades found refuge. David felt like a fugitive but was running away from crimes he hadn't committed. He thought about his problems and then tried to remember the prophecies. Samuel said David would be king, but the reigning king had ordered David's execution. Silently, David wondered if death would pull him from his purpose.

I admit it's hard to have faith in the future when you're fighting through each day. A king may not be trying to kill you, but I am sure some people or situations are trying to distance you from your destiny. Maybe it's a jealous colleague, an ex-spouse, a former friend, or even your mistakes. Sometimes, we are so tunnel-focused on the fight we are blinded from the future, and if we are not careful, the roar of the battle will silence the voice of prophecy.

If we are not careful, the roar of the battle will silence the voice of prophecy.

I've learned that dark seasons tell the truth about our character. In the middle of chaos and conflict, David sowed strength into men who wandered in the wilderness. Those men weren't the guys you find on the golf course but on street corners and prison yards. Reading through David's story, I wondered why God would allow His future king to roam around with a bunch of criminals. Maybe God wanted to see how David would handle thugs and thieves before He entrusted him with the palace. I don't think God forgot about David's future; I think He was shaping David's character for the future.

Epically, David pulled together a band of men who acted like cast members from *The Sopranos*. Somewhere along the journey, the men began to trust David. He gave them purpose, and they offered him protection. They went from crushing kingdoms to constructing one. Within a few months, over 337,000 men found their way to David. This time, the men weren't rouges; they were men filled with wisdom and well-versed in political affairs, high-ranking soldiers armed for battle, and warriors with faces like lions and as swift as gazelles. They had a united purpose—to make David king.

This chapter in David's life is a reminder that dark seasons can have an epic ending.

Although I cannot explain why God chooses specific moments to move in our favor, I trust His plans are better than ours. He knows how to round up resources and position people at the right place and time. Even though we may walk through wilderness places, those paths can lead us to our purpose.

WORDS OF COURAGE

You may be walking through a tough season, but I challenge you not to slump back into what is casual and comfortable. Each of us has a divine mission to carry out. That assignment is far too great to be compromised by false reports of defeat. We must have faith and believe that the strongholds we are staring at can be conquered. When we are convinced that we've been created to save those around us, we will take a swipe at suffering and put an end to injustice. Arise. Step up. Take a swipe at your destiny.

REFLECTION QUESTIONS

God watched how David would deal with three hundred wayward men before He entrusted him with the weight of a nation. What is God trusting you with, and how are you stewarding what He has given you?

Strong leaders can carve purpose out of pain, even when they are the ones who are hurting or grieving. As a leader, do you have a safe circle of friends or a mentor with whom you can talk openly about difficult situations?

David's men became mighty because of his leadership. What personal leadership traits pull people to follow you? In what ways are those who follow you made better because of your leadership?

Sometimes God will let us walk through difficult seasons, so He can round out our character. He knows how much heat we can handle and what trials will make us stronger. If you are walking through a hard season, how are you looking forward to seeing how God will turn things around and bless you despite what you've been through?

____

____

____

____

POWER PRAYER

Father, thank You for watching over me and protecting me from evil. Please give me the grace to lead others, even if they are not likable or agreeable. Show me strategic ways to bring out the best in those following in my footsteps. Today, I believe that supernatural favor and provision are coming my way. Amen.

JOURNAL YOUR THOUGHTS

IMPOSTER SYNDROME

"Have I not commanded you? Be strong
and courageous. Do not be frightened,
and do not be dismayed, for the Lord your
God is with you wherever you go."
—*Joshua 1:9 (ESV)*

While traveling in British Columbia, I decided to go dog sledding. As I climbed into the basket, I asked, "How far can our team run?" The handler replied, "120 miles per day. Stunned, I asked, "How?" He said, "The secret is developing a team where each dog understands their value and place within the team." Pointing, he continued, "See the ones with the red bandannas? Those are alpha dogs; they don't work well with other males, so we place them on teams with females. The trick is to establish a lead dog that will constantly look over its shoulder to make sure everyone is pulling the sled's weight."

As we settled into the basket and began the first leg of the race, I noticed the dog at the back of the pack, Lacy, was running sideways. She was pulling at an angle, almost limping as if wounded. When we stopped, I took the musher aside, "I'm concerned about Lacy. She acts injured. Is she alright?" He laughed, "Yes, she's fine. The truth is she's wired to be a lead dog, but she is still too young to lead, so we put her in the back to learn how to lead at every position. She feels ineffective because she's in the back; therefore, she pulls her neckline away from the gangline and runs to the side. Tugging makes her feel like she is pulling more weight. The trainers laugh at her because she is wasting her energy trying to convince herself she is significant. She will never develop into a lead dog until she can see she is valuable at every position." My heart almost froze at the words. Mentally, I rehearsed them. *Insecure. Doubt-driven. Time wasted—energy depleted.* Lacy sounded like a younger version of myself.

Some of the most successful people suffer from a disorder called *imposter syndrome*. If you are unfamiliar with the term, imposter syndrome is a persuasive feeling of self-doubt or fraudulence despite overwhelming evidence to the contrary.[1] This psychological phenomenon reflects a belief that one is inadequate or a complete failure. It often affects those with high IQs and hits the hardest after achieving a significant accomplishment. If we are not mindful, the enemy of our souls will use the mental and

1 Megan Dalla-Camina, "The Reality of Imposter Syndrome," *Psychology Today*, 3 Sept. 2018, https://www.psychologytoday.com/us/blog/real-women/201809/the-reality-imposter-syndrome.

emotional distortion of imposter syndrome to have us walk away from the very things we are called to do.

WORDS OF COURAGE

Have you experienced the effects of imposter syndrome—thoughts that seek to undermine your worth and diminish your accomplishments? Consider that over 70 percent of people have experienced similar feelings.[2] It is not uncommon for negative internal voices to get stuck in our souls. Sometimes they are the small ones that call out when things get silent; others are the loud ones that lash out for attention. What is important is that we learn how to detect false feelings by identifying voices that are designed to trip us up and drag us away from our callings. I've learned that harmful words, whether spoken by others or by ourselves, have the power to chip away at our confidence.

One way to balance negative and untrue self-analysis is to make a list of personal successes. Highlight ways you have influenced others or altered situations in a positive way. Learn to embrace affirming feedback and be comfortable when you receive recognition for your accomplishments.

---

2 Roslyn Jimenez and Steven Cavazos, "Research Shows 70% of People May Suffer from Imposter Syndrome," *KSAT*, KSAT San Antonio, 9 Jan. 2021, https://www.ksat.com/news/local/2021/01/09/research-shows-70-of-people-may-suffer-from-imposter-syndrome/.

If we are to fulfill our purpose, we must guard our hearts and watch over our souls.

If we are to fulfill our purpose, we must guard our hearts and watch over our souls.

REFLECTION QUESTIONS

Take a moment to evaluate your internal confidence. Think of times when you tried to overcompensate for your insecurities. How did your actions affect your efforts? Whom do you confide in about personal concerns and self-doubts?

____

____

____

Lacy felt invaluable in the story which affected how she performed. What personality traits make you uncomfortable or self-aware? In what ways do your emotions self-sabotage your potential success?

____

On the sledding team, alpha males found working with other dogs with the same disposition challenging. What personality types do you struggle to work with, and why might others find it challenging to work with you?

In what areas of life do you avoid rather than confront your feelings?

PRAYER

Heavenly Father, I ask You to heal my insecurities. Correct my focus, and allow me to see myself the way You see me—valuable and worthy of Your attention. Grant me the grace to live courageously and move forward in confidence. Amen.

JOURNAL YOUR THOUGHTS

LION-HEARTED

. . . The righteous are bold as a lion.
—*Proverbs 28:1 (NASB)*

In parts of Kenya, boys must kill a lion to move into manhood.[3] I know that's hard to believe, but it is true. Numerous documentaries show how Maasai boys will stalk and kill a lion, so they can earn the right to marry a wife. Most of us cannot imagine the pressure of hunting by hand a predator that views us as prey. But the Maasai do not take a casual approach to courage. They believe brave living is the embodiment of adulthood, and courage is grown within the soul and released as situations demand. In the Western world, people are afraid of lions, but in Kenya, lions run at the sight of Maasai warriors.[4]

3 Stephen Scourfield, "Where Lions Are Scared of Men," *The West Australian*, 20 May 2011, https://thewest.com.au/travel/where-lions-are-scared-of-men-ng-ya-168452.

4 Tracey Mitchell, *Becoming Brave* (Nashville, TN: Emanate Books, 2018).

Most of us will never send our children to chase down a lion. But that doesn't mean we don't share in the experience of releasing our children into uncertain circumstances. When I think about women with the same courage as the Maasai, my mind lands on Jochebed, the mother of Moses. Jochebed lived in a barbaric time when Hebrew women were forbidden to give birth to sons. It would be too gruesome to walk you through the backstory, but trust me, Jochebed faced a system more dangerous than lions.

Risking her life and her family, she concealed her pregnancy and gave birth to Moses. That wasn't the end of her courage but the beginning. As months passed and Moses grew, she could no longer conceal the child. She had to make the most daring decision any mother could make. She could risk keeping him, and his enemies might kill him, or she could hide him in the nearby river. History doesn't tell us that lions roamed the banks of the Nile, but crocodiles certainly did. Imagine the courage it took to place her infant son in the water and watch the basket drift out of sight. Only brave-hearted people can trust God on that level. Jochebed added faith to hope and believed that God would take care of her son—or at least send him to someone who would take care of him.

Most parents will never know the horror of their children facing wild beasts. But what about when we are forced to release those we love in other high-risk situations? Maybe war zones, prison, a mission trip, financial risk, or life-threatening surgery. In those pressure moments, do we trust God or resent Him? Faith believes our Heavenly Father will protect the people and things we love from lions and crocodiles or when they are out simply out of our reach.

WORDS OF COURAGE

Being brave isn't just about the big moment or the epic showdown. Courage requires that we prepare for those moments long before they happen. David prepared for Goliath by picking stones out of the brook, the Maasai sharpen their spears before charging lions, and Jochebed handcrafted a basket that would carry Moses. Consider what might have happened in each situation if any of these had failed to prepare. As you go throughout your day, consider how you sharpen or shape your courage.

Being brave isn't just about the big moment or the epic showdown. Courage requires that we prepare for those moments long before they happen.

REFLECTION QUESTIONS

Imagine the tales the Maasai warriors share around the campfire—epic stories about wild animals and daring adventures of conquest. Now, picture yourself sharing a campfire with your closest friends. What tales of courage would you exchange? Would your stories inspire or bore those listening? In what area have you lacked courage?

____

____

____

Revisit the story of David and Goliath (1 Samuel 17). Study how David addressed the battle, his colleagues, and his adversary. How did his words influence and motivate others?

____

____

____

If a stranger were to read through your social media posts, would they think you are a person who has faith or someone who has yet to develop courage? What, if anything, would you change about how you write or talk about difficult situations?

____

____

____

POWER PRAYER

Father, thank You for the challenges that make me stronger and more aware of Your faithfulness. In every situation, I purpose to use words that will minimize my adversity and magnify Your strength. I will surround myself with others who have a warrior's heart. Amen.

JOURNAL YOUR THOUGHTS

FANATICAL FAITH

For no word from God will ever fail.
—Luke 1:37 (NIV)

The ancient books of 1 and 2 Kings are full of miracle moments that make modern urban legends seem small in comparison. If you were to index the miracles in these books, you would find Elijah's name inscribed next to most of them. Elijah wasn't an ordinary faith believer. He was the kind of believer that made kings tremble and armies retreat. His faith was fanatical and his demeanor wild and daring. While other prophets were content to ramble through speeches, Elijah was busy calling fire from heaven and bringing the dead back to life.

I know that it is easy to read right through miraculous moments and miss the weightiness of what happened. That is why I want to zoom in on a piece of a story that is easy to breeze past. I won't walk you through all the backstory that leads up to this moment. Still, to summarize the situation, Elijah stood before King Ahab and spoke this ominous prophecy, "As surely as the Lord lives, no rain or dew will fall during the next few years unless I command it"(1 Kings 17:1, author paraphrase). Let's pause right there.

Only a few people would have the grit to stand before a king and declare a long-term drought. Even fewer have the power to back up a statement like that. Years of drought would mean crops would wither, water sources would dry up, and people would die. That's not the type of prophecy most people stand in line to hear. And it's not the kind of prayer most people want to be associated with. Maybe that's why Elijah hid in the wilderness right after releasing those words. He knew that the prophecy would stir up anger and that the king's army would search for him like they would a criminal.

Elijah prophesied that a drought was coming, and by virtue of the word he gave, he became a participant in that fulfillment. For three years, Elijah depended on a raven to bring him food and a stream to provide him with water. While in solitude, he could have questioned his calling as a prophet; instead, he rejoiced that God kept him alive. The truth was that the national crisis did not diminish his calling but amplified it.

The drought proved that God had established Elijah as a prophet. Three years later, Elijah stood before the king and nation and prayed for rain. The heavens responded, and the flood gates opened at his request. Sometimes, God allows us to be in sticky situations, not because He's against us but because He uses the problem to add credibility to our calling.

Sometimes, God uses a problem to add credibility to our calling.

WORDS OF COURAGE

Sometimes, like Elijah, we have to sit and wait a season out. I am sure it was hard for Elijah to wait in the wilderness with only the birds and wild animals as companions. Imagine the loneliness of being isolated, with no news, no television, or internet, nothing but dead silence. Being in a place of obscurity is especially hard when your dominant gift is interacting with people. But there are times that God will pull us out of our routine so that we can rest and be restored. During those moments, we must remember that sometimes God will sideline us not because He doesn't need us but because He does. He wants us to be at our best before He calls us back off the bench.

REFLECTION QUESTIONS

How does adversity change or shape your identity? Do you feel less valuable when walking through difficult seasons?

____

____

____

When you read of someone with incredible faith like Elijah, where do you think his boldness came from? Would you feel confident declaring an undesirable prophecy to a king or someone who had a significant influence? What tough words has God led you to share with others, and how did they respond to that message?

____

____

____

Read 1 Kings 17. The passage reveals that God kept Elijah safe and protected by the brook until it was time for his next assignment. What were some signs that God wanted Elijah to move somewhere new? Think of a time when God closed one door, whether a job, an opportunity, or a business deal, to lead you somewhere new. How did you initially react to the closed door?

____

____

____

POWER PRAYER

Father, please fill my mouth with Your words, and empower me to speak the truth, even if that means putting my life at risk. Thank You for protecting me in every situation and providing for me even in times of national crisis. Help me hold onto my calling even when times are hard. Amen.

JOURNAL YOUR THOUGHTS

JUST JUMP

Now faith is confidence in what we hope for
and assurance about what we do not see.
—*Hebrews 11:1 (NIV)*

Skydiving wasn't something on my dream list—more like my dread list. Our team wanted to incorporate *Bodyflight* into an upcoming television episode. If you are unfamiliar with *Bodyflight,* it shares many of the disciplines of competitive skydiving like formation and freestyle skydiving. Despite my internal fears, I couldn't think of a reason to reject their idea. I had encouraged our team to think of ways to demonstrate taking risks and stepping out in faith, but I had no idea that would involve a ten-story free fall. Grudgingly, I gave my approval and signed off on the plan.

The flight was scheduled for noon, and I hoped we would be late for or even miss our session. After we made our way through security, we were given safety gear and flight suits. In the simulation room, we met our instructors and were coached on maneuvering through the circulating wind tunnels. I hung on to every sentence as if my life depended on the details.

When it was time to move to the flight chamber, I pushed to the back of our group. I made excuses why I should be the last person to leave the dive platform, and when my turn came, I hesitated. It was all I could do not to turn around and walk away. I kept looking at the tunnel, and the crowd stared at me. Sensing I might bolt, the instructor said, "You're fine. I promise you will be okay. Just jump."

No parachute or hang glider, and the instructor wanted me to *just* jump into a wind tunnel. I was terrified to let go but embarrassed to stay put. Taking a deep breath, I ran to the edge. As soon as my feet left the platform, the wind picked me up, and the instructor grabbed me in midair. Holding on to one of my arms, he went through the signals we had practiced in the simulation room. Slowly, he began to spin me, higher and higher until we were doing free-fall dives and 360 turns against the 150-mph wind.

Before long, I adjusted to the pressure of the wind and learned to control my movements. The longer I flew, the better I became at making the wind take me where I wanted to go. I went from looking like a loose paper wrapper to an eagle using the wind to its advantage. Just as I mastered my movements, the red light came on, and the wind speed slowed. That was my cue to return to base. As I stepped back onto the platform, the weight of gravity returned. Moments before, I had experienced what it was like to live untethered by gravity; suddenly, I felt like an eagle with clipped wings.

On the drive home, I thought about how a leap of faith turned my fears into freedom. I regretted spending so much time on the platform when I could have been soaring.

WORDS OF COURAGE

A leap of faith can feel fatal and freeing at the same time. It is easy for doubt to creep into the corners of our hearts even when we have practiced and prepared and had experts tell us everything will work in our favor. Remember, faith isn't the absence of fear but the moxie to move forward despite fear. Maybe you are standing on the platform of opportunity. Don't let indecision steal away your courage. Take a running leap, fly on the wings of instinct, and let faith lift you to high places.

Don't let indecision steal away your courage.

REFLECTION QUESTIONS

In flight training, I learned how to leverage my body to work *with* rather than *against* strong winds. In what ways can we leverage our faith in aggressive or hostile situations?

____

____

____

____

When was the last time you backed away from an opportunity because you felt anxious or insecure? Would you respond more courageously if you had another chance at the same opportunity?

____

____

____

____

Sometimes the things we dread most lead us to a place of freedom. What dreaded experience turned out to be a blessing? What did you learn about yourself because of the experience?

____

____

____

____

Think through how you approach new experiences. Are you energized by a new challenge, or are you more comfortable letting others go first? What new thing would you attempt to do if you knew no one would judge your efforts? Has perfectionism or social anxiety kept you from leading in certain areas? What talent do you keep hidden because you don't want others to critique your work?

____

____

____

____

POWER PRAYER

Heavenly Father, give me the grace to adjust my attitude toward complex challenges. Help me see that uncomfortable situations are opportunities to stretch and grow my faith. Empower me to lead with confidence and not hide behind others. Amen.

JOURNAL YOUR THOUGHTS

WORDS SHAPE OUR WORLD

The words of the mouth are deep waters, but
the fountain of wisdom is a rushing stream.
—*Proverbs 18:4 (NIV)*

Recently, I was researching the *last words* spoken by famous people. It was interesting to read the various thoughts and expressions that came from someone's soul minutes before they stepped into eternity. Although I didn't hear the words, I sensed the emotion that seeped from the phrases. Some words were light and designed to ease those watching life slip away; others were dark and foreboding as if death were the last chapter. As expected, the *final words* were as varied as the lives of those who spoke them. Some were personal mantras, philosophies, song lyrics, passion phrases, and heartfelt hate. Scanning through the findings made me think of the final words that will cross my lips someday.

I don't know if the story I will share is accurate or folklore. Either way, the report reinforces the concept that our words shape our world. The story claims that a man was hired to repair a refrigerated boxcar near the rear of a train. When he went into the boxcar, he inadvertently locked himself inside. Panicked, he pounded on the door and yelled for help. After hours of his pleas going unanswered, he took a pen and began to journal his thoughts: "With each passing moment, I'm becoming colder. No one can hear me. I feel lost to the outside world."

Hours passed, and the man in the boxcar felt increasingly hopeless. He continued to journal, "There is nothing for me to do but wait. Half asleep, my hands can hardly write." His final entry records, "I feel like these will be my last words." Hours later, they opened the boxcar and found the man had frozen to death. They were shocked to discover the temperature in the boxcar was 56 degrees. The freezing mechanism was broken, and there was abundant oxygen in the boxcar. The medical examiners could find no physical reason for his death. Neuroscientists concluded that he talked himself into dying.

It's one thing to listen to our doubts; it's another thing to empower them with our words.

It's one thing to listen to our doubts; it's another thing to empower them with our words. It may seem far-fetched, but science points to the idea that we are capable of talking ourselves to death. It would be sad if the only reason our viable dreams died were that we wrote their eulogy.

To live fearless, successful lives, we must watch over our words. If words can carry death, they can also bring life. What words have you confessed over your life today? Are they words God would speak over you? Words have creative power. God has given us a mind to envision our future and words to bring those thoughts to fruition. To think one way and speak another is to be double-minded. Today, make a point to say positive words about your future. Ask for supernatural favor. Declare ideas, increase, breakthroughs, and opportunities over your life.

Most importantly, believe you will receive what you request.

WORDS OF COURAGE

As humans, whether we are in crisis mode or in everyday situations, we continually self-evaluate our physical, emotional, psychological, financial, and relational conditions. We repetitiously analyze our feelings and use words to convey our state of mind. Today, try to count the number of times you examine your feelings or circumstances: *I'm not feeling well. Our revenue shares are down today. I am ten pounds heavier than I should be. My wife seems angry at me.* How is constant self-analysis influencing your words, and how are your comments influencing or reinforcing your mood?

REFLECTION QUESTIONS

What would you say if allowed to speak your *final words*? Would those words be congruent with how you have lived? Would they be faith-filled, optimistic, and encouraging or more negative-leaning?

____

____

____

____

Reflect on your thoughts and words. Is your internal dialogue congruent with your beliefs? Do you talk about your future the same way that you would want others to discuss it, or do you minimize the effect of your words?

____

____

____

____

Revisit your childhood and consider how a negative term or phrase affected your confidence. When you remember that moment, do you still feel the impact of those words?

Conversely, have words of affirmation given you the courage to reach for your dreams?

____

____

____

____

Take a moment and construct a list of positive things you want to happen over the next few months. Make sure to include things that may seem illogical or out of your reach. As you make this list, do you find that you are holding back or internally noting why something may not work out as you expect? What Scripture verses are you using to build your faith?

____

____

____

____

PRAYER

Father, please give me the wisdom to pause and think before speaking. Empower me to see the truth about every situation. May my words be a well of life, hope, and encouragement. Amen.

JOURNAL YOUR THOUGHTS

POWER GIFT

Carry each other's burdens. . . .
—*Galatians 6:2 (NIV)*

Empathy may not sound like a power gift, but I have seen a look of compassion heal from a distance. I have watched a nod of hope breathe life into a saddened soul. And I know what it is like for a hand squeeze to express what a thousand sermons could never say.

When we empathize with each other, we tear down walls of emotional isolation.

When we empathize with each other, we tear down walls of emotional isolation. We peel back feelings that say there is no recovery, push against lies that scream at our sanity, and cast out fears that pull up promises before they take root.

People were drawn to Jesus because He noticed them. Contrary to the egocentric society of the modern world, Jesus took time to see and feel the pulse of humanity. The prophet Isaiah gave this description of the Messiah:

> *"The Spirit of the Lord GOD is upon Me, Because the LORD has anointed Me To preach good tidings to the poor; He has sent Me to heal the brokenhearted, To proclaim liberty to the captives, And the opening of the prison to those who are bound . . . To comfort all who mourn."—Isaiah 61:1-2 (NKJV)*

It would be impossible to fulfill this prophecy's beautiful attributes without seeing humanity's condition. One of the identifying marks that Jesus was the Messiah was that no one felt invisible while in His presence. They were fully seen by the Savior.

I've tried to imagine Jesus walking the earth with His eyes locked onto a cellular device, but the thought doesn't feel right. I can't imagine the disciples walking through town snap chatting or at the Last Supper taking selfies. Think of all the miracles that would have gone undone or the needs of people that would have been left unmet if they had been locked into their social media feeds.

Today we are modern-day disciples, and we must ask ourselves, *Are we missing the purpose of serving people by being busy serving ourselves*? We must make sure we are not overlooking the obvious, being absorbed by the superficial.

Living fearlessly isn't always about our courage; sometimes, fearless means pulling others out of their pain or grief. Occasionally, we need to draw our eyes away from our agendas and allow God to show us who needs an extra measure of grace. If you doubt the power of empathy, imagine you are the woman cast at Jesus' feet or the thief hanging next to Him on the cross. Now, look into Jesus' eyes. What do you see? How do those grace-filled eyes make you feel? Maybe we should rethink the restorative power of crawling into the circle of each other's crisis.

WORDS OF COURAGE

During an interview, Naomi Harris was asked to describe the power of human connectivity. Her response still echoes in my thoughts, "It's true about the eyes being the window to the soul. Your face can be etched with worry and twisted by aging, but the eyes tell the true story of who you are."

On countless occasions, Jesus would visually assess people, circumstances, cities, or elements within nature before engaging with them. Scripture reveals He observed His disciples within the context of their daily routines before inviting them to follow Him. He saw Peter and Andrew casting their nets into the sea, and He witnessed Matthew collecting taxes. Jesus looked up into a tree to discover Zacchaeus and looked through the crowd to find the woman with the issue of blood. He was constantly observing humanity to evaluate their physical and spiritual conditions. Today, take a few extra moments to be intentionally aware of others. Ask the Holy Spirit to show you who may need additional words of encouragement or help to get through a difficult time.

REFLECTION QUESTIONS

On countless occasions, Jesus would visually assess people, circumstances, cities, or elements within nature before engaging with them. Consider the many ways He turned ordinary moments into life-altering encounters. What are some ways you could be better at engaging with others?

____

____

____

Have you thought of empathy as being a power gift? What kind of value did Jesus place on empathy? Think of a situation where an act of kindness created a ripple effect of compassion or generosity.

____

____

____

The sight of helpless humanity often compelled Jesus to heal the hurting. When He saw Peter's mother-in-law sick with a fever, He healed her. When He beheld the following crowd's desperation, He was moved with compassion to deliver them of their distress. The sight of Jerusalem moved Him to tears, and the glimpse of a fruitless fig tree angered Him. What emotional triggers spur you to help others?

The influence of social media in our daily lives can be overwhelming. Do you think social media has made you more or less empathetic? Has constant access to the needs of others on social media made you more compassionate or desensitized to others?

POWER PRAYER

Father, thank You for seeing me through eyes of empathy. Forgive me for spending too much time focused on my needs, wants, and desires. Help me be more aware of the pain others are going through, and give me the grace to love like Jesus. Amen.

JOURNAL YOUR THOUGHTS

ALARMS

But the Lord is faithful. He will establish you
and guard you against the evil one.
—2 Thessalonians 3:3 (ESV)

I grew up in rural Virginia, next to a federal correction facility. Living that close to a prison made me cautious of strangers. I had been taught to listen for whistles that would let the public know when an escaped convict was on the loose. I would soon discover that sirens don't always announce strangers. Sometimes, those who are sent to trouble us come silently and without warning.

When I was ten years old, I was flipping through a magazine we received in the mail. I noticed a picture of a bearded man holding a crucifix and a giant green frog attached to the cross. Beneath the cross was the caption, "He died for your sins."

The image made me so upset that I cut it out and placed it on a bulletin board in my bedroom.

A few months after saving the photo, I heard a stranger's voice coming from our living room. Curious, I went to see who the voice belonged to, and when I rounded the living room corner, my heart almost stopped. There, sitting on my couch, was the bearded man who had been holding the crucifix.

He said, "I heard you have a picture of me. Can I have that picture?" My face went pale, and I lost control over my words. The only thought that tumbled through my mind was, *How did he find me?* I know you want to know the rest of the story, but it would take too long to unravel in this short space. Just know that individuals linked to the occult had visited my home weeks before and had let the man know I had his picture.

I tell you this story as a reminder that agents of heaven and hell know your address. The kingdom of heaven and the forces of darkness will send situations and people across your path. Sometimes, those moments will come with a great announcement, and others will creep in silently.

As God's plan for your life unfolds, be mindful of who is interested in your future. When God began to work in David's life, the prophet Samuel came to his house, and King Saul summoned him to the palace. Samuel offered David a prophecy, and Saul offered David a position. Those were strange but defining moments for David. There will be defining moments in each of our journeys. If we live out our days unscathed and without scandal, we must discern the motive behind the message and distinguish who will help us and who will hurt us.

We must discern who will help us and those who will hurt us.

WORDS OF COURAGE

In every season of life, the enemy of your soul will test your resolve to remain faithful to your callings and dreams. He will strike in unsuspecting ways and through unlikely people. When you feel like you will fail, remember that your adversary cannot steal what you are unwilling to surrender. If you are weary, pray. If you are fearful, confess the Word over your future. Above all, contend for your faith. God has a plan that is greater than any scheme of the enemy. When we follow the words of our Father, we win. Take time to ask for wisdom, reach forward confidently, and be quick to obey.

REFLECTION QUESTIONS

Sometimes it can be hard to distinguish the intentions of others. Think of a time when you were caught off guard by the wrong motives of someone you trusted. When you are unsure about someone's character, do you pause and ask God to reveal the heart of others, or do you rely on your instincts?

___

___

___

Have you felt called to go in one direction and then had another opportunity try and pull you away? What excuses, if any, have you made for not fully committing to what God is calling you to do?

___

___

___

Think of a friend or colleague who always makes the right choice. How do they go about making their decisions? What steps do they take to safeguard their reputation?

___

___

___

PRAYER

Holy Spirit, may our ears hear what heaven is saying this season. Give us discernment to know whom to align ourselves with and whom to move away from. Cover us with divine protection, and keep us from harm.

JOURNAL YOUR THOUGHTS

STILL STANDING

For the righteous will never be moved;
he will be remembered forever.
—Psalm 112:6 (ESV)

The Leaning Tower of Pisa is a famed landmark in Italy that attracts five million visitors annually. Even though I understand the sacred representation of the prayer tower, I can't help but tilt my head in disbelief. Walking through an art gallery, I stared at a painting of the tower and thought the structure looked like a wedding cake baked by a seven-year-old. The architect in me wanted to level the foundation, push the walls upright, and make them parallel.

If you've been to Italy or taken a modern art class, you probably know that the facts about the history of the tower are vague. Some historians claim the tower was funded by Pisans who pillaged the city of Palermo and wanted to create a *field of miracles* to show off treasures gained from their conquests.[5] Other accounts claim that a local widow, Donna Beta di Bernardo donated sixty silver coins to kick-start the construction. All historians agree that they cannot identify who created the original architectural plans for the tower. Maybe that is a good thing. I doubt many people would want their name inscribed on the slanted structure.

Pisa is a Greek word meaning "marshy land." Maybe that was the clue the architects overlooked because the tower began to sink before the second floor was completed. The three-meter limestone foundation was too shallow to support the 14,500-ton tower.[6] The design was flawed, but no one was brave enough to call off the construction. Rather than abandon the project, engineers continued to build. Every time a story was added, the engineers would try to stabilize the structure by compensating in the opposite direction. As a result, the exterior lean has changed directions multiple times, and the interior is a maze of walls and rooms of dramatically varying heights and shapes. After 849 years, the world's finest engineers have yet to balance or permanently stabilize the tower.

Maybe the tower entices so many visitors because it symbolizes their personal lives in myriad ways. Like a landmark of

---

5 Gina Mussio, "11 Things You Didn't Know about the Leaning Tower of Pisa," *Walks of Italy*, 3 Oct. 2016, https://www.walksofitaly.com/blog/art-culture/leaning-tower-of-pisa-facts.

6 Ram Jack, "The Foundation of the Leaning Tower of Pisa," *Ram Jack*, 22 Sept. 2015, https://www.ramjack.com/houston/about/news-events/2015/september/the-foundation-of-the-leaning-tower-of-pisa/#:~:text=The%20foundation%20was%20made%20of,sinking%20in%20on%20one%20side.

courage, the tower silently tells each generation that a flawed beginning doesn't mean you have to give up or deconstruct. Even though it can be hard to believe, sometimes, your mistakes or imperfections are the things God will use to make you stand out. Consider that hundreds of thousands of towers exist worldwide, but one of the most identifiable is the one that is still being worked on.

WORDS OF COURAGE

Imagine looking at a high-rise building. On one side of the structure is a wrecking ball, and on the other is a crane. Unless you have a copy of the blueprints, it may be hard to tell if the building is going up or if it is being torn down. Maybe there are situations in your life that resemble the building. Some people advise you to keep building, and others encourage you to tear it down and start over—the tension of trying to decide while under pressure can feel overwhelming. If you find yourself torn between people's opinions, I encourage you to hit the pause button and pull away. Find a place to be alone and hear what God is telling you to do. He is the Divine Architect. He knows the things that will hold together and the things that will fall at the first round of fire.

REFLECTION QUESTIONS

Consider a time when you pushed forward with an unstable plan. What was the driving factor of your decision, and why were you so determined to move ahead? How much time or energy did you waste trying to straighten out something that should not have been built?

____

____

____

____

When things don't work out the way you plan, are you quick to quit, or do you bring on experts who can balance out your mistakes? What expert advice have you invested in, or whom have you collaborated with in the last six months?

____

____

____

____

What personal relationships or business deals began with a shaky foundation? How did that instability affect what you were trying to build?

____

____

____

____

The Leaning Tower of Pisa represents change, grit, and resilience to some people. In your life, what situation or relationship embodies those character traits?

____

____

____

____

POWER PRAYER

Father, thank You for holding me together when I feel like falling apart. I rest knowing that You will smooth out my foundation and fortify the walls around my heart. Please show me when I need to balance out my thoughts or change my attitude. May I have the grit and grace to withstand change. Amen.

JOURNAL YOUR THOUGHTS

INVINCIBLE

For the Spirit God gave us does not make us timid,
but gives us power, love and self-discipline.
—2 Timothy 1:7 (NIV)

The other day, I scrolled through an internet blog and stumbled upon a woman's story that shook me to my core. Her name is Dr. Susan Richards, and she is a fictional superheroine. Through an interesting turn of events, Susan received supernatural powers after exposure to a cosmic storm. I know it sounds strange, but the storm gave Susan the gift of invisibility. Once Susan survived the storm, she could slip into obscurity. Whenever she wanted to blend in or slide into the shadows, she would use the power the storm had brought to disappear and disengage.

By the time Susan encountered the storm, she had already survived her mother's tragic death and her father's imprisonment. She was forced into dark and damaging situations, including her involvement with a man who was utterly psychotic. After the storm, she said, "I know a lot of other things now. Things I've been trying to put aside, to postpone. The Psycho-Man did more than twist my emotions. He forced me to look into the deepest corners of my soul, forced me to confront who I am, what I have become." She explained, "When we gained our powers, we lost something. An innocence. A child-like naivety. For a long time, I've tried to go on as if . . . I was still the same. But I'm not. Not after all that's happened to us, not after what the Psycho-Man did to me. There is no Invisible Girl anymore. . . !"[7]

Even though Susan is fictional, most of us can relate to the idea of wanting to be invisible. I am sure there are moments we would like to disappear or at least cast a force field around those we love and protect them in our most vulnerable moments. But that kind of power and protection doesn't come to us until we have gone through and survived epic storms—until we've had to walk through dark seasons and make hard choices and been forced to decide whether the storm will define us or destroy us. Those are the make-or-break moments that will determine whether we come away a heroine or simply hurt.

Storms make us vulnerable. What we decide to take away from those moments of vulnerability and the voices we choose

---

7 "Fantastic Four, Volume 1, 284," *Marvel Database*, https://marvel.fandom.com/wiki/Fantastic_Four_Vol_1_284.

to amplify during those shell-shocking seasons will determine whether we walk out of the storm invincible or morph into an invisible state. Those are our two options: being invincible or walking through life invisible.

Visualize the invisible.

WORDS OF COURAGE

As I travel, men and women share personal stories of how a crisis affected their identity. I have noticed how people interpret and respond to problems is marginally different. While some grudgingly fight through situations, others use crisis as a catalyst for change. Those who fight to find positive outcomes in stormy seasons discover opportunities that others overlook.

Crisis is a catalyst for change.

If you are experiencing significant life stressors, look at how those pressures alter your identity or influence your relationships. Consider that unexpected change can be beneficial. Sometimes, we need the extra push to grow, evolve, and dive deeper into our purpose. Gaining a better understanding of who we are will help us mature into the best version of ourselves.

REFLECTION QUESTIONS

If you're experiencing a major life crisis, what steps are you taking to guard your faith? Are you reaching out for emotional support or wisdom from trusted advisors?

____

____

____

____

How do you handle unexpected stress? Do you tend to suppress your emotions or allow them to erupt? What are healthy ways you can work through unexpected stressful situations?

____

____

____

____

Susan's identity changed as a result of the storm. Have difficult situations altered how you perceive or embrace your strengths or weaknesses?

____

____

____

____

PRAYER

Heavenly Father, I ask for Your strength to guide me through difficult seasons. May I look to You for comfort, wisdom, and peace. Please teach me how to be invincible when I want to be invisible. Amen.

JOURNAL YOUR THOUGHTS

WILD DISCOVERY

"O Lord, please open his eyes that he may see."
So the Lord opened the eyes of the young man,
and he saw, and behold, the mountain was full
of horses and chariots of fire all around. . . .
—*2 Kings 6:17 (ESV)*

I'm an adventurist. I love exploring exotic places and experiencing different cultures. My friends will tell you if the risk isn't a part of what we are planning, then we probably won't do it. Reading up on remote locations, I discovered a long list of intriguing, if not mysterious, places to stay. I found igloo lodges in northern Norway, an underwater resort in the Maldives, cliff-hanging outposts in Peru, and even futuristic capsules in Japan.

Probing deeper, I widened the travel sites to include more historical landmarks. The search led me to Xi'an, one of the most popular destinations in the world. Xi'an became a famous landmark after Chinese farmer Yang Zhifa found ancient history buried in his orchard. In 1974, Yang's shovel struck something solid while he was digging a well. At first, he thought it was pottery or a large stone, but he notified local authorities when he realized he had discovered something significant.

Chinese architects made a wild discovery. Under Yang's orchard were massive burial pits depicting the armies of Qin Shi Huang, the first Emperor of China. The life-sized Terracotta Army included more than eight thousand vividly painted soldiers, some standing six feet tall and weighing 450 pounds. Also entombed were 130 engraved chariots and 670 sculpted horses[8] with infantry soldiers, chariots, cavalry, bronze carriages, and weapons.[9] According to one source, Xi'an is the world's largest heritage site, extending more than 25 square miles.[10]

It would be hard for most of us to imagine that a massive army could be buried in our backyard, that an entire system of soldiers, chariots, and horses could lie inches beneath the surface. Maybe that is how Elisha's servant felt when an invading army surrounded them. The young man could see the enemy's forces but was oblivious to God's army. Aren't there times we

---

8 Jane Portal, *The First Emperor: China's Terracotta Army* (Boston, MA: Harvard University Press, 2007).

9 M. Martinon-Torres, "The Warriors of Xi'an," National Geographic History, May/June 2021, 46-59.

10 M. Martinon-Torres, "The Warriors of Xi'an."

all fall into that trap? We are acutely aware of our enemies but blindly oblivious to divine intervention.

In the book of 2 Kings, Elisha asked God to take the blinders off his servant's eyes. He wanted him to be able to see things from heaven's perspective. To look at things from a divine dimension and experience the holy awe of visualizing the invisible. God granted Elisha's requests, and what his servant saw was more spectacular than a sci-fi movie; it was a celestial army with horses and chariots of fire. That same army surrounds us today. Just because we can't see something with our natural eyes doesn't mean it doesn't exist. I pray that, like Zhifa and Elisha's servant, we discover that armies are all around us.

WORDS OF COURAGE

The Oxford Dictionary defines revelation as the divine or supernatural disclosure to humans of something relating to human existence or the world.[11] If we are to avoid the traps and pitfalls that are designed to destroy us, we must seek revelation every day. It requires that we set aside time to block out distractions, rise above the chaos, and step into heavenly realms, so we can receive supernatural instructions.

11 "Revelation English Definition and Meaning," *Lexico Dictionaries* | *English*, Lexico Dictionaries, https://www.lexico.com/en/definition/revelation.

REFLECTION QUESTIONS

Sometimes a crisis can cloud our vision and blind us from the truth. If God were to reveal hard truths to you, would you embrace or ignore them?

Thinking back to Yang's story, reflect on your past experiences. Have you ever unearthed information or stumbled upon a situation that others have hidden? What did you do with what you discovered, and how did it impact others?

In the story from 2 Kings 6, Elisha asked God to open his servant's eyes, so the servant could see things in a spiritual context. In this story, are you more like Elisha, who sees things through the lens of faith or the servant who tends to focus on the circumstances?

In what area do you need revelation? In what environment do you hear God's voice the clearest?

____

____

____

____

POWER PRAYER

Father, thank You for protecting me in every situation. As I lean in and listen to Your voice, show me opportunities I would otherwise overlook. Program my heart to pay attention to things my natural eyes cannot see, and adjust my vision to see issues from a divine point of view. Amen.

JOURNAL YOUR THOUGHTS

ASK FOR THE IMPOSSIBLE

There has never been a day like it before or since, a day when the LORD listened to a human being. . . .
—*Joshua 10:14 (NIV)*

Tucked away in the book of Joshua is a story that I don't think gets enough attention. It is a tale so fascinating that history archives it as, "There has never been a day like it before or since, a day when the Lord listened to a human being." Stop and read that sentence aloud. It sounds like a lead line that would make a screenplay writer salivate. But that phrase wasn't from some mystery novel or a blockbuster film. No, that line was written by the man who lived the real-life version of the story. And he chronicled the events that took place that day as the zenith, the high point of all history.

If we aren't familiar with the events, the skeptic might think the writer was playing up the drama or taking creative license to embellish the tale. He didn't. If anything, the scene was underplayed. Rather than have you read the extended version of the story, let me give you the highlight reel.

The story opens with Israel's troops surrounded by five opposing armies. In a gutsy move, Israel's leader Joshua did the unexpected. Instead of waiting to be attacked, his militia stuck first. After traveling during the night and fighting a fierce battle all day, the sun began to drop, and darkness encroached. Frustrated, Joshua looked at the sky and knew that victory might elude them if his army didn't finish the fight that day. They were desperate for the one thing no human could control, more time. Again, the story is so short that it doesn't fill in all the details. Maybe Joshua purposefully documents the events with the same tempo that they lived them—sudden, quick, without careful detail or planning.

With the last seconds of daylight fading, Joshua circled his troops and revealed his strategy. Wait for it. It was not a military maneuver, a battle plan, or a covert operation. Joshua's plan was a prayer. It was a prayer that had never been prayed because no one thought it could be done. With everyone waiting and listening. According to Joshua 10:12 (NIV), Joshua stretched his arms to heaven and made an outrageous appeal, "Sun, stand still over Gibeon, and you, moon, over the Valley of Aijalon."

That command was perhaps the wildest and fanatical order to cross a human's lips.

Joshua didn't ask God *if* the sun could stand still; he asked God to *make* the sun stand still. And according to his request, "The sun stayed in the middle of the sky, and it did not set as on a normal day. There has never been a day like this one before or since, when the LORD answered such a prayer" (Joshua 10:13-14, NLT).

WORDS OF COURAGE

The stronghold of insecurity has been downplayed, if not overlooked, in our culture. Over and over, the media communicates a message of doubt, encouraging people to be cautious and live anxiously. The downside of doubt is that it clips the wings of our faith. Unknowingly we cling to what is comfortable, settle for small dreams, and retreat into obscurity. It is time we shatter messages that morph our faith and crush our courage. We need to live like Joshua and pray prayers that generations will remember.

It's time we shatter messages that morph our faith and crush our courage.

REFLECTION QUESTIONS

Some who heard Joshua pray must have thought he was out of his mind or at least not thinking clearly. What risky prayers have you prayed that made others believe you had stretched your faith too far? After reading this story, do you feel you need to pray with greater expectations?

____

____

____

When you find yourself in a situation where you may run out of time or resources, does prayer become part of your victory strategy? What is the greatest prayer you've seen answered? How did the answer to that prayer encourage others?

____

____

____

I'm sure you've heard people pray long and rambling prayers, or maybe you have spoken some yourself. The interesting thing about Joshua is that he asked for one of the greatest miracles in history, yet his prayer was only a few phrases long. What can Joshua's request teach us about praying intensely and intentionally?

____

____

____

POWER PRAYER

Father, I long to offer up prayers that others will marvel at generations from now. Thank You for showing me that You are not insulted by irrational prayers or put off when we ask for the impossible. As I learn and grow, may I see that believing in the supernatural is a normal way of life. Amen.

JOURNAL YOUR THOUGHTS

DIMENSIONAL VISION

We look not to the things that are seen but
to the things that are unseen. . . .
—2 Corinthians 4:18 (ESV)

A few months ago, I had trouble with my vision, so I scheduled an appointment with a new optometrist. Once I was in the examination chair, he placed the phoropter machine in front of my eyes. After a few turns and clicks, he said, "Oh, I see you're Irish."

Caught off guard, I push back in the chair. I had to consider whether he was a doctor or a stalker. I asked, "How do you know that? That information isn't on my chart." His response amazed me, "I can tell your heredity by the shape of your iris. Your history is responsible for shaping your vision."

Your history is responsible for shaping your vision.

The phrase, "Your history is responsible for shaping your vision," stuck in my mind.

Intrigued, I did what every research journalist does: I googled the information to see if he was right. I found that over two thousand distinct genes create intricate and unique iris patterns.[12] Studies show that our iris patterns are more accurate in proving identity than our fingerprints. Consider that we unlock our cell phones through biometric facial features rather than fingerprints. As I continued researching how heredity influences vision, I realized that our vision is not only a projection of what we see but how we are conditioned to see ourselves and the world around us.

Neuroscientists claim that Leonardo da Vinci had a visual impairment that allowed him to see the world with dual depth perception, an ability most creative people would love to experience. The study claimed his impairment, which likely caused one of his eyes to turn outward, enabled da Vinci to switch between bidimensional and tridimensional vision.[13]

---

12 "Iris Patterns," Iris Patterns | *AncestryDNA® Traits Learning Hub*, https://www.ancestry.com/c/traits-learning-hub/iris-patterns.

13 Scotty Hendrix, "Leonardo Da Vinci Could Visually Flip between Dimensions, Neuroscientist Claims," Big Think, 26 Oct. 2018, https://bigthink.com/health/da-vinci-eye-problem/.

Although the impairment could have proven a disadvantage, it made da Vinci a dimensional genius. He created numerous scientific inventions, further evolved physiology and anatomy, and invented flying machines, helicopters, parachutes, and large-scale crossbows. His flaw empowered him to see what others were unable to envision.

My thoughts lingered on the topic of dimensional thinking. If one man's natural impairment allowed him access to a multidimensional world, what could God do with impairments if we placed them in His hands? Sometimes what we consider a liability is simply an unrecognized asset. The things you have been calling dirt could be your diamond.

This year, consider praying the words of Job, "Teach me, what I do not see" (Job 34:32, NKJV).

WORDS OF COURAGE

One glance through history reveals world changers are those who are courageous enough to think differently. Da Vinci's colleagues likely thought many of his inventions were far-fetched or an overflow of his self-indulgent imagination. Perhaps, like many thought leaders of our generation, he was labeled eccentric or unconventional. I am sure many considered da Vinci's philosophies scandalous, the kind of concepts that would ban one from Twitter if that were a thing in the fourteenth century.

> Thankfully the da Vincis of this world don't hide their creativity or talents in the corner—nor should we.

REFLECTION QUESTIONS

How has your history or personal experience shaped how you see the world? Think of a friend or family member who views situations differently. How can you see that their experiences shape their choices or decisions?

____

____

____

____

Da Vinci used personal impairment to his advantage. If you had total self-confidence, what weakness would you transform into a strength? What would be your dirt to diamond?

____

____

____

____

People often hold on to ideas and viewpoints from childhood or young adulthood. What mindsets do you need to consider changing if you are intentional about personal growth?

____

Consider that you may think or act differently when around various groups of people. How do the opinions or actions of others influence your perspective?

PRAYER

Father, please show me how to find creativity in chaos. Let me see that my uniqueness is valuable. Give me the courage to see things and people in a fresh light. Amen.

JOURNAL YOUR THOUGHTS

FEARLESS NOT FOOLISH

Those who trust their own insight are foolish,
but anyone who walks in wisdom is safe.
—*Proverbs 28:26 (NLT)*

Spades and shovels chinked against the stone rubble. The archeological site was mysterious and foreboding. Breathtaking, it was like a backdrop from a sci-fi movie. The ruins held a secret, and the secret was more heartbreaking than the modern world could imagine.

Excavators worked cautiously as historians and students of antiquity watched in wonder. After 1,600 years, the ancient Roman city of Pompeii was uncovered and brought back to life. As if death were frozen in time, Pompeii had been preserved as it existed when Mount Vesuvius erupted in 79 AD. Considered one of the greatest natural disasters in history, scientists speculate that the volatile eruption expelled hot ash, deadly gases, and molten rock more than twenty-one miles high and released one hundred thousand times the thermal energy of the atomic bombings of Hiroshima and Nagasaki.[14]

Walking through the ruins of Pompeii was like being teleported in time. Eerily, the archeological dig revealed buildings still intact, skeletons frozen where they had fallen, and everyday items like jars of preserved fruit and loaves of bread undisturbed in their original places. There were other details, small ones that told stories of everyday life and large foreboding ones that seemed to warn future generations.

Seeing the graphic images of Pompeii made me question the wisdom of the citizens who built their homes within five miles of the base of the volcano. Although the villas offered elaborate mountain and seaside views, the foundation was unstable, and the ground gave warning signs of unrest. It is reasonable to wonder, *Were they unaware of the impending danger or so comfortable that they ignored the warning signs?*

It is hard to imagine a society being so careless that it would build its infrastructure on something that had the potential to destroy its citizens. But that is what the residents of Pompeii did; they gave in to their *wants* instead of paying attention to the *warnings*. They were fearless but in a foolish kind of way. They invested in comfort and gambled on security. Today, the ruins of Pompeii serve as an unpleasant warning. As if time-stamped

---

14 "Man of Pompeii," *Time*, 15 Oct. 1956, https://time.com/.

by history, the remains silently beg future generations to pay attention to the foundation.

Mt. Vesuvius has erupted a dozen times since that fateful day in 79 AD and is still one of the most dangerous volcanoes in the world. Even with geologists warning of a future eruption, 3.5 million people live within twenty miles of the volcano's crater. One must consider if the risk is worth the reward of a seaside view.

WORDS OF COURAGE

The Romans' passion for owning a piece of paradise left them oblivious to the obvious. They built villas for *beauty* with no thought to *balance.* The artisans constructed courtyards and made mosaic masterpieces but overlooked the simple act of examining the foundation. I wonder how often we, like the people of Pompeii, push through warning signs while pursuing our passions. I admit it is easy to get caught up in the beauty of what we are creating and miss the subtle signs that may safeguard our dreams down the road.

Subtle signs may safeguard our dreams down the road.

REFLECTION QUESTIONS

The ancient city of Pompeii remained hidden for 1,600 years. What memories or tragedies have you intentionally tried to forget? Would you have the courage to unearth those memories and allow others to receive healing from your journey?

____

____

____

____

What are your emotional *blind spots*, and how do they influence your decisions?

____

____

____

____

Has a fear of missing out on a *once-in-a-lifetime deal* clouded your judgment? How did you deal with the pressure of instant gratification?

____

____

____

____

Consider a time when you took a calculated risk to achieve a professional goal. What were the tradeoffs? What was the outcome?

PRAYER

Heavenly Father, thank You for ordering my steps and guiding me away from dangerous situations. Please give me discernment to see things and people the way You see them. May I build my dreams on Your Word and principles. Amen.

JOURNAL YOUR THOUGHTS

WINDOWS OF HEAVEN

Therefore I tell you, whatever you ask for in prayer, believe that you have received it, and it will be yours.
—*Mark 11:24 (NIV)*

Magicians are notorious for making things disappear. In New York City, I watched con artists pull watches right off people's wrists. And I have seen theatrical productions where illusionists made birds vanish, cards disappear, money turn into smoke, and assistants fade from the stage. The entertainment industry is good at hiding what already exists. But one has to turn to Biblical history to witness the creation of things that never existed.

Reading through the book of 2 Kings, I found a passage that would make modern magicians shudder. The backdrop of this setting reveals that the ancient region of Samaria was in such an economic collapse that animal heads were being sold at premium prices, and the citizens had turned into cannibals.

I know that is graphic; it makes my stomach turn, too. But I want you to sense the gravity of the situation. It wasn't just a recession; it was a national scourge.

With kings threatening the lives of prophets, Elisha made a prophecy that within twenty-four hours, the economy would be completely turned around, and lack would be replaced by abundance. Hearing Elisha's announcement, 2 Kings 7:2 essentially reports that the king's assistant said, "That couldn't happen even if the Lord opened the windows of heaven!" But Elisha countered, "You will see it happen before your eyes, but you won't be able to eat any of it."

I cannot imagine making a prophecy of that magnitude. Elisha wasn't saying that something was going to disappear or go away. No, he was forecasting the impossible—the divine reversal of a nation's economy—not over a long period but within a day. If I lived in Samaria, I might have been tempted to doubt also. But Elisha had built a resume out of seeing the impossible take place.

Build a resume on seeing the impossible take place.

In a tale that is too dramatic to believe, the unthinkable happened. Four starving lepers went to the camp of the opposing Aramean army to surrender. When they arrived at the military site, it was ominously abandoned. The lepers fumbled through the darkness and found abundant silver, gold, cattle, and clothing. They would later discover that God had made the Aramean army hear sounds of galloping horses and speeding chariots and a vast army approaching. And just as Elisha prophesied, there was a divine reversal of fortunes.

As for the king's assistant who doubted, he was trampled to death as the people rushed out to receive the miracle. Elisha's words held; the man saw the miracle but never partook of it.

WORDS OF COURAGE

I cannot tell you the times I've heard about miracle moments that faded all too quickly. The truth is most people find it easy to receive from God but struggle to keep favor flowing through their lives. Consider that it is possible to receive the blessings of God and never hold on to them. Managing what heaven releases in our lives is not God's responsibility—it is ours. Being a steward of the harvest is just as important as reaping it. Today, be mindful of what has already been entrusted to you. Watch over it. Manage it. Multiply it.

REFLECTION QUESTIONS

Read 2 Kings chapter 7. Given the economic condition of Samaria, would you have believed the words of Elisha? Do you think God wants to do the same kind of epic miracles in our generation?

____

____

____

____

How would you feel if a modern-day prophet set a time limit on when a prophecy was to come to pass? Would you hold them accountable for those words if they were not accurate?

____

____

____

____

Reading through the story, why do you think God used lepers, who were the outcasts of their society, to receive the miracle? Do you think others immediately believed their story, or did it seem too good to be true?

____

____

____

____

Reflect on the fact that God only had to use a sound to create a miracle. Sometimes, when we try to imagine how God will work a miracle, we complicate the scenario. Think of a time in your life when God used something simple to do a great work. Did His plan or strategy surprise you?

____

____

____

____

POWER PRAYER

Father, thank You for sending unexpected miracles my way. Help me see that You have the power to turn horrible situations around. Today, I choose to activate my faith and stand ready to receive good things from You. I do not want to miss anything that You have for me.

JOURNAL YOUR THOUGHTS

FOLLOW THE PLAN

Commit your way to the LORD; trust
in him, and he will act.
—*Psalm 37:5 (ESV)*

As we lingered over coffee, Michael began to talk about Sharon's financial earnings. The multimillion-dollar portfolio was impressive, but what silenced the table was the revelation that Sharon's company contributed eighty percent of its profits to humanitarian projects and charitable organizations. When we asked Michael how Sharon built a real estate empire in a few years, his answer sounded like fiction, but the story was true.

After decades of marriage, Sharon's husband unexpectedly passed away. After his death, she paid off existing debt and had a few thousand dollars in her savings account. Because Sharon hadn't attended college or worked outside the home, she had no idea how she would financially hold things together.

Alone and afraid, she spent hours walking and praying. She specifically asked God to give her creative and innovative ideas. Her prayers were answered, but not in a way she could have anticipated.

In a dream one night, a voice said, "Sharon, I want you to go into business." Immediately, she argued with the voice and said, "I don't know how to manage a business, and I don't have the capital to launch a business." The voice said, "Sharon, all I am asking you to do is follow my plan. Will you allow me to be your business partner?" Shocked and confused by the invitation, she cautiously agreed and said yes. When she said yes, she awoke from the dream.

A few weeks later, Sharon noticed a small property near her house was for sale. Hesitant, she called the real estate agent and asked for the purchase price. She wrote down the price and prayed over the land. Feeling the property was linked to her dream, she bought the lot and dedicated it to God. Within sixty days, the property sold, and she made an extraordinary profit.

Sharon took the profit from that transaction and bought another parcel of land. She flipped that property for triple the price, continued to buy and sell real estate, and amassed a small fortune. One day, the banker in her small town pulled her aside and asked if she had a silent business partner. She laughed and said, "I have a business partner, but He isn't silent. When God speaks, I follow His plan."

God doesn't reserve divine strategies for a handful of people. He has extraordinary plans for each of our lives. Although our

Father is the Architect of the universe, He also holds custom blueprints for our destinies. He longs for our partnership and to be included in our decisions.

We must follow the blueprints of the Divine Architect.

WORDS OF COURAGE

Angles and altitude have a way of shaping our perspective. If you have taken a commercial flight, you understand how different things look from thirty-two thousand feet. At ground level, things that may seem enormous or unconquerable suddenly look bit-sized and achievable from a lofty cruising altitude. The same is true with how we see our situations, problems, or challenges compared to how God views them.

Angles and altitude shape our perspective.

Aerial views provide a better overview than what earthly glimpses deliver. That is why it is crucial to rely on God's wisdom. He doesn't make decisions based on a limited perspective, but He sees the entire canvas—mountains, valleys, peaks, and pits—and knows how to guide through the terrain.

REFLECTION QUESTIONS

The more comfortable and settled we are, the harder it can be for us to obey God's voice. If God spoke to you in a dream or some other way, would you be willing to uproot your life and start something new? Would you be quick to follow that opportunity, or would you drag your feet?

____

____

____

____

Like a roadblock on a freeway, sometimes situations in life force us to take new routes or go in a different direction. When unexpected change comes your way, are you irritated, or do you choose to be positive, versatile, and optimistic?

____

____

____

____

When you pray, do you ask God to show you situations and people how He sees them, or do you try to get God to view things your way? An excellent way to check your perspective is to evaluate whether your views align with Scripture. Ask yourself the hard questions. Is this how Jesus sees this person? Are my circumstances guiding me, or am I letting faith lead the way?

____

____

____

____

PRAYER

Father, I promise to pay attention to the signs and dreams You send me. I will lean in and listen to Your voice when I am tired or confused. Instead of relying on my strategies, I will be quick to agree with Your plans. Thank You for the added benefits and rewards that come from serving You.

JOURNAL YOUR THOUGHTS

GIANT DECISIONS

The naive believes everything, But the sensible person considers his steps.
—*Proverbs 14:15 (NASB)*

The other night, I found an old storybook in the garage. As I flipped through the pages, my eyes fell on the story of "Jack and the Beanstalk." I'm not sure what made me read back through the tale, but I am glad I did. The more my thoughts lingered on the story, the more I became convinced that the fable was created for executives rather than children.

If it has been a while since you read the story, I will refresh your memory with a few details. Jack was a hard-working farm boy, but he and his mother went hungry every night. One day Jack decided to sell his cow, Bessy, so he could buy seeds and grow a harvest. On the way to town, Jack met a charismatic man who offered to give him magic beans in exchange for

Bessy. He promised Jack, "If you plant the seeds overnight, by morning, they will grow to the sky." Jack made the deal, went home, and tossed the beans out of his window. The following day, exactly as the man promised, Jack's seeds grew into a stalk reaching the sky. Inquisitive, Jack climbed the stalk, and at the top of the stem was a castle filled with gold.

The man failed to tell Jack that a giant who liked to crush small children was guarding the gold. It occurred to Jack that getting the gold wasn't worth fighting the giant. He realized that he had grown something that had the power to destroy him. Panicked, Jack raced from the castle, but the giant followed him. Jack understood the only way to stop the giant was to chop down the magic stalk.

As I closed the book, I thought about how sometimes, we don't notice the enemy's trap until we are standing inside it. A few years ago, I was tempted to take a shortcut to success. Late one evening, I received a call from a talent agency on the west coast. They asked if I could meet with their representative in Dallas to discuss how their company could represent my work. Excited by the opportunity, I rearranged my schedule and drove to Texas. I wish I could tell you I spent hours praying before leaving home, but I didn't. If I had been paying more attention to the inner nudge of the Holy Spirit, I would have never agreed to walk into that meeting.

The offer they made me was more lucrative than I could have imagined. It wasn't for thousands; it represented millions. As I reached for the deal, my heart sank, and my peace left. In a way that is hard to explain, I felt like the oxygen had been suddenly sucked out of the room. Looking back at the opportunity, I realize I could have quickly fallen into a trap so strong that I could never have pried my way free. God protected me by pulling back His peace. I learned that not everything that entices us away from God's perfect plan appears evil. Sometimes the trap is set in a way that seems neither good nor bad . . . simply convenient.

WORDS OF COURAGE

Research estimates that people make thirty-five thousand decisions every day.[15] Reading that statistic makes my mind spin at the possibilities. Thinking about the ripple effect of one decision is enough to neutralize our thoughts or keep us from acting. That is especially true if we have been stung by the blowback of a wrong decision. Whenever our team arrives at an adverse outcome, we quickly evaluate how a better result could have been achieved. Post-decision analysis is healthy and constructive and prevents repetitive mistakes.

Take a moment and consider the principles that are found in Jack's story. Contemplate that Jack shouldn't have negotiated with a stranger whose character had

15 Eva M. Krockow, "How Many Decisions Do We Make Each Day?" *Psychology Today*, Sussex Publishers, 27 Sept. 2018, https://www.psychologytoday.com/us/blog/stretching-theory/201809/how-many-decisions-do-we-make-each-day.

not been tested. Think through the pitfalls of deals that have the potential to grow too soon; often, *once-in-a-lifetime deals* can be dangerous if not lethal. I know this last thought is heavy, but consider what you would do if you created something that had the power to destroy you. Would you consider taking back that power or shutting it down altogether?

What would you do if you created something that could destroy you?

REFLECTION QUESTIONS

Fatigue and stress can pressure us into making off-the-cuff decisions. What is your approach to making decisions when you are physically or emotionally drained?

____

____

____

____

In the story, Jack was too young to be making life-altering decisions. Do you know of young men or women who would benefit from your counsel? How are you using your expertise to better someone's life?

What impromptu or pressing decisions have created blind spots in your judgment? When faced with a hard decision, what scriptures do you rely on to sharpen your focus?

PRAYER

God, reveal any traps or pitfalls that cross my path. Please protect me from making unwise decisions that could adversely affect my future. May I find the courage to take the right route, even if that way seems slow or difficult.

JOURNAL YOUR THOUGHTS

SLIGHT SHIFT

Trust in the Lord with all your heart and lean not on your own understanding; in all your ways submit to him, and he will make your paths straight.
—*Proverbs 3:5-6 (NIV)*

In 1983 Korean airliner 007 took off from New York City, headed to Anchorage, Alaska, and then to Seoul, Korea. When the plane left Anchorage, there was a slight flight plan error of about one degree. Because no one caught the mistake, the plane went further away from its intended destination. That small miscalculation would determine the fate of the 269 passengers on board. Flight 007 inadvertently flew into Russian airspace and was shot down by Soviet fighter jets, and everyone on board perished.[16]

16 "Korean Air Lines Flight 007," *Encyclopædia Britannica*, https://www.britannica.com/event/Korean-Air-Lines-flight-007.

It doesn't seem fair that a minor miscalculation would be powerful enough to determine the fate of one's life, but it happens all the time. Research reveals that most people don't fail to reach their goals by a gaping margin; on average, people miss their goals by less than one degree. Somewhere along the journey, they get slightly off course, and because they refuse to recalibrate, change, or adjust their approach, they fail to achieve their intended results. They travel further off the path, and the longer they wait to adjust, the harder it is to get back on track.

On average, people miss their goals by less than one degree.

If we reverse engineer our way through history, we will find that subtle nuance or slight shifts transformed entire cultures. A one-degree intellectual shift often revolutionized the world. The Greeks applied philosophical reasoning and altered how the world approached problems. Darwin's theory of biological evolution distorted the Biblical worldview of creation. Martin Luther's *Ninety-five Theses* changed the context of how the believers viewed faith and were the catalyst for the Protestant Reformation. I know these are broad examples of how an idea can create a ripple effect of change, but if a thought has the power to change the world, imagine how it could transform your life.

While writing these words, I think about how easy it is to drift off course and casually compromise our principles or bend our theology to appease culture. If we are not mindful, the slight slip-ups will pull us from our purpose over time. A moment of anger, a night of unguarded passion, a lapse in judgment, or an unhealthy relationship has the power to change the course of our lives. Now let's take that word of caution and move it in an affirming direction. Consider that a slight adjustment in our thinking could empower us to push forward with our dreams, motivate us to live a healthier lifestyle, or stimulate us to pursue a goal we've shelved. Think about the books you are reading or the podcasts you are listening to and how they guide or influence your life. Remember, over time, small changes yield significant results.

WORDS OF COURAGE

In science, a temperature change can alter a substance's structure. Consider that at 32 °F, water takes on a solid form, at 33 °F, it liquefies, and at 212 °F, it transforms into steam. While the molecular properties of water remain the same, its shape or structure is influenced by atmospheric conditions. A temperature shift can affect form, substance, consistency, and conformity. In the same way, our lives are shaped by our environment. If situations in your life are moving or veering in the wrong direction, consider what external influences are impacting your present and future.

REFLECTION QUESTIONS

Take an honest look at your life. What minor miscalculations took you away from your goals or intended destination? How were you able to adjust and get back on course?

In what area of your personal life or business do you lack accountability? What steps are you taking to build future accountability?

Do the books you read or the podcasts or streaming platforms you subscribe to challenge you to think deeper or encourage you to pursue your dream? What thought or idea has created a ripple effect of change in your life? Are you making a positive impact in the lives of others? If so, how?

PRAYER

Father, help me slow down and listen to Your voice. Show me when I am getting off track or missing the mark. Help me stay on the path that You have designed for my life. Amen.

JOURNAL YOUR THOUGHTS

OPEN DOOR

. . . When he opens a door, no one can close it, and when he closes it, no one can open it.
—*Revelation 3:7 (GNT)*

This year, I am passionate about making sure I don't miss what God is doing. I don't want to ignore an instruction, overlook a divine opportunity, or miss a chance to be a part of a miracle. As I searched for scriptures for this new year, I stumbled upon a verse that shook me out of my spiritual slumber.

Turning through the sticky pages in Revelation, my eyes landed on Revelation 4:1. Before I reveal the secrets contained in that verse, let me paint a verbal word picture of what had transpired in the previous chapter. In chapter three, God showed John the condition of the churches. God highlighted the churches' strengths and revealed their weaknesses in great detail. Then it was as if God suddenly changed the conversation. Maybe you've had those moments with God, too. When it seems like you are following along with what God is showing you, you suddenly discover that God has made a quick turn and is talking about something else.

After discussing the condition of the churches, God redirects the conversation and gives John a divine invitation to come up higher and see things in another dimension. He allows him to see futuristic events, mysteries that only those standing in the heavenly realm had access to. John recorded the moment this way:

> *After this, I looked and saw a door that opened into heaven. Then the voice that had spoken to me at first and that sounded like a trumpet said, "Come up here! I will show you what must happen next."—Revelation 4:1 (CEV)*

Imagine the holy awe of being called up, invited to stand in the heavenly realm, and given insider information on what will happen next. God called to John just like He is calling to our generation, saying, yes, there has been chaos and confusion, and there is a list of things the church hasn't gotten right yet. But never forget that there is an open door in the heavenly realm for those willing to come up higher. Think about how liberating those words are. We have grown accustomed to the difficulties that accompany opportunity. However, imagine a door that isn't boarded up or sealed shut—a door that is unlocked and standing wide open.

This year God is calling us to come up higher. He is inviting us to awaken from our lethargy, turn off any distractions that would keep us from hearing His voice, and enter into a realm where we receive divine instructions and inside information.

WORDS OF COURAGE

We often get so caught up in the chaos of what is going on in the world that we overlook the unique opportunities that God sets before us. It would be heart-wrenching to come to the end of our lives and realize that we spend our best days focusing on things that do not matter. Today, journal your thoughts. Pay attention to what you are thinking about. Evaluate whether you are spending the majority of your time worrying about things you cannot control or if you are taking time to rise above the chaos and see things from a heavenly perspective.

Rise above the chaos, and see things from a heavenly perspective.

REFLECTION QUESTIONS

Sometimes we need to evaluate if we have become the *architect* of our lives or if we have reserved that role for the *Architect of the Ages.* Are we directing our lives or allowing the Holy Spirit to lead and guide us through each day? Are the dreams we are pursuing ours, or were they God-inspirited?

____

____

____

When was the last time you invited God to show you things from a heavenly perspective? We live in a media-saturated society. Comparatively, what percentage of your time do you spend watching news reports, reading blogs, or listening to a podcast? What amount of time would you be willing to commit to prayer and reading God's Word?

____

____

____

Most people don't have a hundred prayer requests they want to be answered, but they usually have two or three needs that stay at the top of their list. Look at your prayer list. Which requests would you like God to answer first? This week as you pray, as God to give you divine instructions. Believe that the things that have been locked up tight will be opened, and the things that have been held hostage will be released.

____

____

____

POWER PRAYER

Father, thank You for giving me access to Your kingdom. I don't take the initiation to come up higher lightly. Today, I will design my schedule and prioritize my time with You above everything else. Please show me the hidden mysteries of Your kingdom and grant me inside information concerning what is next on Your timetable. Amen.

JOURNAL YOUR THOUGHTS

RISE UP

Without counsel plans fail, but with
many advisers they succeed.
—*Proverbs 15:22 (ESV)*

Some accomplishments are easily achieved; others are born in the trenches of adversity. In the mid-1800s, the city of Chicago grew into a major lake port and industrial center. The city was built on marshland, and massive amounts of mud made the infrastructure unstable. Because the city was only three feet above Lake Michigan, underground sewers did not drain properly, and the streets filled with toxic waste.[17] Contaminated water and unsanitary living conditions fueled an outbreak of cholera that killed 5 percent of the population. As a modern-day comparison, the city of Montreal has a

17 "The Time They Lifted Chicago Fourteen Feet," *Enjoy Illinois*, 3 Dec. 2018, https://www.enjoyillinois.com/illinois-200/raising-chicago/.

combined urban population of 7.5 million. A loss of 5 percent of the population would equal 375,000 deaths.

Some accomplishments are born in the trenches of adversity.

With one in twenty dying, the city of Chicago searched for ways to dig beneath its foundation and stabilize the infrastructure. In a mass effort, city leaders attempted to solve the problem by grading the streets, so water could run into the river. When the grading process failed, they planked over the roads only to have moisture decay and decompose the make-shift foundation.

Feeling defeated and out of ideas, city officials consulted with Ellis S. Chesbrough, an engineer from Boston. An innovative thinker, Chesbrough recommended the illogical. Since efforts to dig beneath the city had failed, he suggested elevating the city. I am sure this advice made those in the room take a collective breath. Raising a city block would seem a tall task; elevating the entire city would appear impossible.

Few believed that Chicago could rise out of the ruins. Others speculated that even if the mission worked, it would bankrupt the city. But the critics misjudged the character and grit of the citizens. For two decades, work crews used thousands of large jackscrews to raise the city four to fourteen feet higher than its foundation. The engineering feat of raising the city without collapsing the infrastructure was a modern miracle.

Chicago received global attention as the world watched in wonder. When the renovation project was complete, Chicago had one of the country's first comprehensive stormwater and wastewater systems.[18] In two decades, Chicago went from sinking in sewage to a city celebrated for progress and innovation. Those who discovered themselves in a desperate situation found the courage to reinvent their surroundings and build stronger, better lives.

WORDS OF COURAGE

Finding healthy solutions to our problems doesn't always happen overnight. Sometimes, we need to step away from our challenges and allow others to submit their ideas or offer insights that might have been overlooked. Whether raising a family, growing a business, or launching a new project, we need innovative thought leaders who see things from a different perspective.

There will be crucial moments when we must decide whether to take a risk or wait out the storm. Those heavy types of decisions don't come easily or without forethought. One of the things I admire about Chesbrough

18 Sarah Zhang, "Chicago Was Raised over Four Feet in the 19th Century to Build Its Sewer," *Gizmodo*, 26 Sept. 2016, https://gizmodo.com/chicago-was-raised-more-than-4-feet-in-the-1800s-to-bui-1646409024.

was his ability to create change without destroying the infrastructure of what had been previously built. I admit that it's not always easy to navigate change and keep things intact. Take a few moments and consider how a city pulled together and pulled out of a seemingly impossible situation. Now apply that same level of ingenuity and determination to your situation.

REFLECTION QUESTIONS

The leaders of Chicago needed the wisdom and engineering expertise that Chesbrough brought to the table. Who do you consult with or lean on when things are difficult? Is your team open to new ideas or collaborative work sessions?

____

____

____

Are you facing a problem that seems to have no solution? Have you considered ideas that may be far-fetched or unrealistic? Are you willing to take significant risks that might affect your career or level of influence? Would you take the advice of someone like Chesbrough?

____

____

____

Does your family or close circle of friends adapt well to new ideas? How can you help someone who is resistant to change expand their way of thinking?

____

____

____

What illogical idea has made a positive change in your life? Were you quick to embrace the concept, or did it take a while to warm up to it? Do you feel that you need to embrace new ideas at a faster or slower rate?

____

____

____

POWER PRAYER

Father, thank You for innovative ideas and divine strategies. Please unlock my imagination, so I can see opportunities even when encountering adversity. Fill my mind with wisdom, knowledge, and understanding. Amen.

JOURNAL YOUR THOUGHTS

WHAT IF

. . . Our LORD, make the sun stop in the sky . . . and the moon stand still. . . .
—*Joshua 10:12 (CEV)*

Lately, I have been reading about great "What If" moments in history—the kind of philosophical exploration that imagines how things might have turned out *if* history had happened differently. For instance, what would have happened if Alexander the Great had lived past thirty-two? Would he have achieved global conquest, and would the world have one language and religion? Would World War II have happened if a priest hadn't saved four-year-old Adolf Hitler from drowning? The counterfactual list of things that almost, should have, or might have occurred under different conditions is endless.

Counterfactual thinking may seem like a waste of time if you aren't a big fan of historical facts. But before you turn away from this kind of exploration, consider the great "What If" moments of the Bible. What if Judas hadn't betrayed Jesus or Eve hadn't reached for the forbidden fruit? I understand that those far-fetched theories are too much for most of us to think through. But what about less-dramatic moments when small decisions would have determined how a situation turned out? Consider what might have happened to David if he had fought in Saul's armor. Would David have won? Would we even know about David?

Small decisions have the power to change the trajectory of our lives. Sometimes, it's not until we are on the other side of those choices that we experience the consequences of our actions. I feel sure that if Jonah could have turned back time, he would have gone straight to Nineveh. Achan would have never stolen silver. Ananias and Sapphira would have told the truth. Abraham wouldn't have slept with Hagar.

But not every story in history needs a counterfactual outcome. Some situations happen as they should, and some people get things right the first time. When Joshua's army needed a miracle, he didn't ask God *if* the sun could stop, he asked God to *make* the sun stop and the moon stand still, and God did what Joshua asked. Imagine the euphoria of that moment. There's no way to improve the story; it couldn't have a better ending. What about us? Do we have epic moments of faith that we wouldn't dare let counterfactualists rewrite? I hope we all have audacious moments of faith when we believe in the incredible and contend for the impossible.

Believe for the incredible, and contend for the impossible.

WORDS OF COURAGE

In life, we don't always make the right decisions or choose the best path. It is easy to look back on a situation and wonder *what if* I would have handled things differently. *What if* I would have taken time to weigh my words or stop something before it got out of hand? Honestly, we all have moments that we wish we could take back or redo. While regret may ease our conscience, it doesn't move us forward in life. Today, take inventory of your thoughts. Instead of living from a place of regret, think of ways faith can make you stronger.

REFLECTION QUESTIONS

If you knew you only had a few months to live, would you spend time languishing over regrets, or would you embrace the time you had left?

Consider the words that you use to describe your future? Are those words reckless and damaging, or do they portray passion and enthusiasm? If you met someone like you, would you think they are critical or too hard on themselves?

In what areas of life are you most discouraged? When you think about your future, do you envision yourself making the same old mistakes, or do you dream of doing something fresh and new?

POWER PRAYER

Father, I bury missed opportunities, shortcomings, or failures in the past. I refuse to live in the graveyard of yesterday, but with great expectation, I look forward to the future. Please help me stop criticizing my past so that I can celebrate the good things that are coming. Amen.

JOURNAL YOUR THOUGHTS

FINISH STRONG

I have fought the good fight, I have finished
the course, I have kept the faith. . . .
—*2 Timothy 4:7 (NASB)*

I wouldn't define myself as a rock jock, but I am an avid backpacker who enjoys climbing rough terrain and some low-lying mountains. Wanting to read up on some challenging treks, I found an article about the perils of climbing Mount Everest. Embedded in a list of facts was an interesting statistic that revealed more people die descending the mountain than ascending. The article explained that more than two-thirds of the tragedies happen after mountaineers reach the world's highest summit peak. Climbers tend to get enraptured with the notion that they have reached their goal and forget the most dangerous part is still ahead of them.

According to Bill Burke, the oldest American to summit Everest, "A lot of people don't have the energy and reserve to make it down, and they get a sense of euphoria and become careless. You need to keep your concentration at all times. You can't let your mind wander. Climbing Everest is a round-trip endeavor."[19]

Bill's words stuck in my soul. I began to think of how often people develop a strategy, launch a project, or dive into a dream only to lose energy halfway through the journey. Or worse, some discover that they should have never taken on the task. Maybe that is how Sarah felt when she watched Abraham embracing Hagar's baby bump. Suddenly her plan read like a poorly written script. Halfway through the process, she wanted to push the pause button and rewind what she had set into motion. But there wasn't a pause button, and she was forced to finish what she started.

I've learned that God doesn't bless all of our plans, and when God's favor is not on our actions, our dreams can turn into nightmares. It's unlikely that many of us will get hung up climbing off a mountain, but what if we get stuck halfway through our dreams? How do we pull ourselves together and find a way to finish what we've started? Sometimes, the first step to getting unstuck is to pray about the next move. I know that may sound obvious, but it's something many forget to do.

---

19 Alyssa Roenigk, "Layering, Gummy Bears and 5g -- What We've Learned in 100 Years on Mount Everest," *ESPN*, 4 May 2021, https://www.espn.com/espn/story/_/id/31359749/layering-gummy-bears-5g-learned-100-years-mount-everest.

It would be hard to count the number of cragsmen who made a fatal step because they didn't secure the rope when belaying. Similarly, prayer and spiritual disciplines are the ropes that keep our spiritual feet from slipping. Faith tethers us to truth and secures our steps when we must work our way out of perilous situations.

Faith tethers us to truth and secures our steps.

WORDS OF COURAGE

Think of prayer as an opportunity to draw God's goodness into your chaos. As you pause and humbly ask for help, God opens the windows of heaven and releases words of encouragement. He is faithful to give you divine plans, strategies, and words of wisdom that will empower you to cross the finish line. Whatever crisis you encounter, remember to make time for small prayer breaks. Embrace quiet, reflective moments. Unlock the windows of heaven with your words of faith and adoration.

REFLECTION QUESTIONS

Do you feel like you have started something that you cannot complete? Create a timeline that will help you determine how you arrived at this feeling of hopelessness. If a close friend were in a similar situation, what words of wisdom would you offer them?

____

____

____

Take a moment and think about how you pray. Do your prayers tend to be more confident or hesitant? What hard thing would you ask God to do if you knew the answer to your request would be yes?

____

____

____

Are you currently stuck in a situation because you made a wrong decision? Meditate on the story of Sarah in Genesis 16-21, and consider that God blessed her even when she felt trapped by her actions.

____

____

____

POWER PRAYER

Father, teach me to pray in faith, without doubt or holding back. Even now, I will begin to make audacious requests knowing that You desire to bless me and enlarge my influence. I trust that You have good plans for my life; even though I cannot see them, I know they are moving toward me. Amen.

JOURNAL YOUR THOUGHTS

FIX YOUR FOCUS

Let your eyes look directly forward, and
your gaze be straight before you.
—*Proverbs 4:25 (ESV)*

Last year, I decided to take surfing lessons while on vacation in Hawaii. Surfing the waves at Waikiki Beach was something I had always envisioned doing. I had no surfing experience but was optimistic and determined to master the board in a single session.

My instructor's name was Bear, and he called me Mitchell. I am sure he regretted pulling my name from the list. I'm a perfectionist—the kind of tourist instructors dread coaching. In an annoying way, I challenged every instruction that tumbled off Bear's lips. It wasn't that I didn't have faith in his abilities; I doubted mine.

Paddling away from shore, I yelled, "What if I can't get up on the first try?" Bear replied, "Children are the best surfers.

They have no fear and don't experience performance anxiety. Relax Mitchell. Just keep your eyes on the horizon and fix your feet. Don't overthink."

Telling me not to overthink was like asking a bird not to fly. Overthinking was instinctual.

Paddling harder, I asked, "What if a wave sideswipes my board?" In a voice used to calm a child, he said, "No matter what comes up, focus forward. Forget everything you think you know. People that bring previous experiences or negative thoughts with them fail.

I kept analyzing, "What happens if my board rocks?" He yelled, "Stand up straight. Don't try to balance yourself. If you tighten up, your weight will shift away from the board, and you will wipe out."

As we settled in where the waves began to rise, I asked, "What if I get tired?" He leaned back on his board and said, "The hardest part of surfing is paddling. Don't use your strength to fight through a wave; leverage the top of the board, and it will carry you over it."

Bear's words lingered in my heart long after the sun fell beneath the sky. I thought about faith and doubt and the spiritual application of my experience. If we are brave enough to swim in deep waters, waves of doubt will rise around us. If we don't keep our eyes of faith fixed on what is before us, we will lose our balance, and waves of doubt will drag us under. But if we relax, focus, and maintain our balance, the rhythm of our faith will lift us above the doubts and carry us safely to shore.

WORDS OF COURAGE

Living in a time when chaos and confusion abound, we have to learn to steady our hearts and emotions. If we are not mindful, doubts will minimize our confidence and drown out our desire to think big and embrace audacious dreams. But this is not the time to drown in a pool of hesitation or be swept away by the current of cares. This is our season to swim into deeper waters and make brave our new normal.

Swim in deep waters, and make brave your new normal.

REFLECTION QUESTIONS

Think of some historical and Biblical stories that deal with the topic of overthinking. How does being overly analytical slow us down or work against our faith?

____

____

____

____

If you had an instructor like Bear, do you think you would respond well to his coaching style?

____

____

____

____

How have your previous experiences impacted your confidence in trying new things?

____

____

____

____

PRAYER

Father, forgive me for doubting Your Word. Please help me to stop overthinking and living from a place of anxiety. I know that my future is secure when my eyes are fixed on You. Give me the courage to rise in faith and confidence. Amen.

JOURNAL YOUR THOUGHTS

REWARDS OF WAITING

In the morning, LORD, You will hear my voice; In the morning I will present my prayer to You and be on the watch.
—*Psalm 5:3 (NASB)*

Digging through my office closet, I found an old journal. As I flipped through the pages, my eyes landed on a prayer list that was highlighted, circled, and starred. In the margin, the ink was smudged, and the page was thin where tears had seeped through the paper. As my fingers traced the words, my memory drifted to a time when I desperately needed those promises to come to pass. I'm sure I am not the only one who has pressed their Bible beneath their pillow and fallen asleep holding on to hope.

Holding on to a dream can be daunting—the paradox of being drawn to it but fearing it. Wanting something but not wanting to experience the pain of wanting it. The deep yearning of hoping things will happen and the monotony of waiting, watching, and waiting again can unsettle the bravest warrior.

I am sure Hannah felt unsettled when she went to the temple to pray. She wanted to wash away the bitter feelings of another woman holding her husband's child. Hannah needed room to take her shoes off and stand somewhere sacred. To pull in and plant her face in the soil where priests heard from God. To soak in the atmosphere where she felt her prayers would make it past the ceiling. To unload longings that were turning into strongholds and release the heartbreak that was building into bitterness.

Maybe, like Hannah, you have felt the sting of having someone walk around with your dream. An unholy rival stole something that belonged to you; perhaps it was land that belonged to your family, a house you planned on buying, an idea for a book, or a business plan that would have made millions. Whatever it was, they took ownership of your dream as if it were theirs.

I admit that I've walked through seasons where bitterness tasted sweet—until it didn't. I specifically remember when I had to pry my hands off a situation, so God could give me something more significant. Letting go wasn't easy, but I knew that bitterness was a barrier and that God-sized dreams don't grow in the incubator of unforgiveness. During that time, God brought Hannah's story to mind. The Holy Spirit reminded me her womb had been sealed shut, not because she was unworthy but because she was chosen to carry a prophetic child. Her womb wasn't barren; it was reserved. Was she forced to wait and suffer pain? Yes, but she would eventually experience the rewards of waiting, trusting, and believing. Her son, Samuel, would live with priests, walk with kings, and change the course of history.

WORDS OF COURAGE

The crib remained empty ten years after God told Abraham he would be a father. No baby. No hint that a child was on the way. It wasn't like they were in their thirties; Abraham was one hundred years old, and Sarah was ninety. If you read their story carefully, it's easy to see they agonized over a child while not understanding God wanted to give them a nation. If the waiting process is any indication of how prophetic promises play out, then perhaps the length of your delay is a sign of the size of your destiny. Stop underestimating God's power and plan. Wait with expectation.

The length of your delay is a sign of the size of your destiny.

REFLECTION QUESTIONS

How do you react when the elevator doors don't close quickly? Do you impatiently bang on the buttons or wait a few seconds? What do you do when Google doesn't give you the answer you were looking for? Do you nervously tap on the screen or retype your search? Does reacting impatiently move things along or make us more agitated? How does waiting on spiritual promises compare with how you approach delays or setbacks in your daily activities?

____

____

____

____

Think of a hurtful situation—maybe a close friend or colleague stole a plan or idea that was important to you—but later, it led to a better plan. Did that experience help you see that God can turn negative situations around, even use them to propel you further ahead?

____

____

____

____

In Scripture, many powerful women like Sarah, Elizabeth, Hannah, Rachel, and the mother of Samson struggled with conceiving a child. Eventually, when the time was right, they gave birth to prophets, priests, kings, and warriors who would change history. If you knew that something incredible was in your future, would you be willing to wait on it with patience and grace?

____

____

____

____

POWER PRAYER

Father in Heaven, thank You for protecting my life and safeguarding my dreams. As I move forward into a new season, I decree that Your limitless favor will go before me. Today, I release feelings that would hold me back and embrace Your plan of victory. Fill me with peace, and allow me to see the good things that are in my future. Amen.

JOURNAL YOUR THOUGHTS

EPIC EMOTIONS

But he must ask in faith without any doubting,
for the one who doubts is like the surf of
the sea, driven and tossed by the wind.
—James 1:6 (NASB)

Walking through the Dallas Museum of Art, I felt drawn to a work composed by French artist Francois-Auguste Biard. The painting captured a ship tossed about at sea, and from the dramatic pitch of the bow, the boat appeared to sway back and forth, lurching and turning with every swelling wave. As I took time to study the masterpiece, I noticed the detail Biard used to capture the expressions of the passengers; some looked panic-stricken and others serene. Some appeared proud and aloof while others seemed weak and terrified. Each passenger seemed to overlap into another space as people were shown collapsing into each other's arms while others pushed against each other as they attempted to stand upright. The contrast of emotions spilled across the canvas in a gripping way.

The cohesive factor in the artwork was that it was chaotic and disordered. As I looked closer, I noticed the paradox of events: men stood in the center of the frame smoking, a baby appeared calm, a monkey climbed out of a box, and a young gypsy asked for donations while the ship could be sinking. I slumped back in my chair when I realized the genius of the work. Artistically, Biard used chaos to create a sense of continuity.

As I left the museum, the emotional effect of the masterpiece stayed with me. My thoughts drifted to another storm when twelve men were cramped in a small boat on the Sea of Galilee. Most of us are familiar with the story, so I won't give too many details. But imagine the fury of the tempest. Use your senses to connect with the scene. Visualize dark clouds on the horizon and feel the spray of the waves rising from the sea and spilling over the bow and stern. Notice the torn sails and the broken mast; then, look closely at the faces of the other disciples. They are etched with anxiety and engraved in fear. At that moment, the only thing binding the crew together was the mutual feeling of chaos in crisis.

Think of the last time you found yourself in a storm of epic proportions. Maybe it wasn't a literal storm but an emotional, relational, or financial one. What emotion would the world see if that moment was time-stamped and freeze-framed? If Biard had painted the expression on your face, would it be one of faith or fear, and would you want the world to be left with that image? Consider that our faith and fears spill across our faces when we think others aren't looking.

WORDS OF COURAGE

Just because we may lose sight of our faith for a moment doesn't mean we cannot come back stronger. Once Jesus delivered the disciples from the storm, they began to trust Him more deeply. Sometimes, our weaknesses need to be highlighted to find ways to strengthen them. Take time, and consider Biblical leaders like Moses, Peter, Samson, and the apostle Paul who once made poor decisions but repented and went on to achieve great things for God.

REFLECTION QUESTIONS

Applying a counterbalancing technique, Baird used the backdrop of a storm to capture the diversity of human reactions when they are thrown into harm's way. What troubling scene has created various reactions within your close circle of friends? How did differing or opposing reactions affect your relationships?

____

____

____

Each of us positively or negatively influences people who are watching us walk out our faith. Do you think others are drawn to or pushed away from your beliefs based on your actions and reactions during crisis moments?

____

____

____

If you have to walk through a difficult season with others scrutinizing your actions, do you tend to withdraw or publicly push forward? Think of those in the Bible who kept positive attitudes in grave situations. What steps did they take, and how did they respond when publicly ridiculed or accused?

____

____

____

POWER PRAYER

Father, thank You for being faithful to me even when I have been unfaithful to Your plan. Today, I am determined to focus on You even when dark clouds gather and the storm rages. I refuse to give up or walk away from Your will just because things don't work out the way I hope the first time. I declare I am walking into a new level of faithfulness. Amen.

JOURNAL YOUR THOUGHTS

CARRYING DREAMS WITH EASE

Do not be anxious about anything, but in everything by prayer and supplication with thanksgiving let your requests be made known to God. And the peace of God, which surpasses all understanding, will guard your hearts and your minds in Christ Jesus.
—*Philippians 4:6-7 (ESV)*

Mitchell ran in the door and slung her backpack on the table. She tugged on the zipper and then grabbed a fistful of balloons. Excited, she asked me to get the *balloon machine* out of the closet and watched in wonder as the air began to round out the balloons.

She yelled, "Bigger . . . make the balloons bigger."

Wanting to please her, I continued to push the balloon down on the nozzle.

Smiling, she chanted, "Bigger . . . is better."

On the fourth push, the balloon burst.

Her face fell, and she asked, "What happened?"

I said, "Baby, there was too much pressure."

Confused, she tilted her head and asked, "Pressure? What's pressure?"

Pause. Great question. How do you explain the effects of pressure to a four-year-old?

I said, "Pressure happens when too much air is forced into a small space. . . ."

Nodding as if she understood, she handed me a balloon and said, "Do another one . . . but this time . . . not so much pressure."

What a great perspective. A do-over with less pressure. I am sure that if we were allowed to do seasons of our lives over, we would make profound changes. Lately, I've thought about how our drive to *have more* or *do more* often pushes us past what is healthy. Our quest to be more influential, purchase a larger building, or have a more extensive financial portfolio can create unmanageable tension.

To lead fearless lives and work from a place of confidence, we must manage internal and external pressures. It does us no good to bravely reach for our goals only to self-implode or emotionally crash and burn.

When I think of influential people who were daring and successful, my mind immediately drifts to Joseph. One of the things that I admire about Joseph was his ability to lead a nation through difficult times without scandal, emotional collapse, or burnout. Like any other leader, Joseph was placed in a pressure chamber of expectations. Within moments of being installed in office, Joseph had to construct a plan to sustain a nation through economic uncertainty. The difference between Joseph and some leaders is he understood how to release the pressure to God. He wasn't interested in being famous; he was addicted to being faithful. Because his motive was to please God, the stresses that could have crushed him became easy to carry.

Joseph wasn't interested in being famous; he was addicted to being faithful.

WORDS OF COURAGE

It would be unreasonable to think dreams are fulfilled apart from pressure. Good things happen, but they usually come with stress or at least a considerable amount of tension. Many of the world's great leaders developed their grit by going through situations others would try to avoid. I've found that confidence isn't usually born out of comfort; it is a trait gained from surviving seasons of abandonment, criticism, or false accusations. If you are working through a hard season, remember that the strength you are developing today prepares you for great things in your future.

REFLECTION QUESTIONS

Most everyone has goals they want to achieve, but sometimes, reaching for them can create surprising amounts of stress. If you repeatedly feel overwhelmed, what are healthy ways you can stabilize your peace? What healthy boundaries do you have in place to help guard your peace?

____

____

____

____

Last year, many top-earning CEOs resigned from their positions without warning. They listed frustration, fear, and changes within the culture as core contributors to their decisions. What underlying issue could potentially push you to make significant life changes?

____

____

____

____

Sometimes, people try to avoid fulfilling their responsibilities by delegating those tasks to others. Do you feel taken advantage of when others try to push their work off on you? Are you comfortable with saying no to things you do not feel are your responsibility? Make a list of ways you would feel comfortable saying no, and use those phrases as needed.

____

____

____

____

POWER PRAYER

Father, I know You are ready to absorb my sorrows and relieve my tension. Therefore, I will not sink into stress or collapse under pressure. Through Your grace, I am prepared to take on the toughest challenge. Thank You for giving me the strength to do what You have called me to achieve. I look forward to finishing strong. Amen.

JOURNAL YOUR THOUGHTS

DIVINE PLANS

"The thief does not come except to
steal, and to kill, and to destroy.
I have come that they may have life, and that
they may have it more abundantly."
—John 10:10 (NKJV)

Reading through Scripture, I couldn't help but notice the number of times death threats were attached to significant moments in history. The list of prophetic events that were paired with assassination plots and foul play makes me uneasy. Although sketching out the details of those stories would take up too much time, I want to highlight a few episodes that reveal the gravity of what I am referring to. Consider that when Nehemiah went to find out about the condition of Jerusalem, death threats were slipped under his door. Similar experiences happened to other mighty leaders like David, Esther, Jeremiah, and Paul. And as gruesome as it sounds, when Moses was conceived, the king of Egypt issued an edict to kill the male children when they were born. Herod reacted the same way when he found out about the birth of Jesus, but his regime didn't stop at the murder of newborns. Over and over, the pattern remains the same; the enemy of God's kingdom will attempt to wipe out divine plans before they are set into motion.

In today's culture, most of us aren't physically threatened, but our dreams get fired on, or our plans end up in the crosshairs of an enemy. Maybe I am different, but I cannot remember when I attempted to do something significant for God, and things came together smoothly. I wish I could tell you that things supernaturally fall into place when you serve God, but I don't want to mislead you or give you false hope. Sometimes, we have to fight to keep things from unraveling even before they get started.

Sometimes, we have to fight to keep things from unraveling even before they get started.

A few years ago, my husband and I bought a new home. Three days after we signed off on the deal, the unthinkable happened. My husband had gone on a business trip, and I had gone shopping for furniture. When I returned home, I unlocked the side door and walked to the back of the house. Halfway across the room, I froze in horror. The back door was smashed in, and glass was scattered across the floor. Within seventy-two hours of owning our home, we had been robbed. Even though police searched the grounds and assured me that I was safe, I felt violated and cheated out of the joy of our new home.

For days, I kept a gun strapped to my side and jumped at every noise. I was sure I would never feel safe again. But then I remembered God had strategically and miraculously moved us to Dallas. When I listed off all the miracles that happened to make that transition possible, I began to see things from a new perspective. Instead of allowing the intrusion to discourage me, I decided to view the break-in as confirmation that we were exactly in the place where God needed us.

WORDS OF COURAGE

Consider committing these verses to memory:

The LORD *looks* down from heaven
and sees every person.
From his throne he *watches* all who live on earth.
He made their hearts and understands
everything they do . . .
But the LORD *looks after* those who fear him,
those who put their hope in his love.
—*Psalm 33:13-15, 18 (NCV, emphasis added)*

REFLECTION QUESTIONS

Have you been intimidated by the opposition that comes with doing something for God? Do you feel like the resistance is greater than the grace of God? If not, what is keeping you back from doing the thing that is in your heart to accomplish?

____

____

____

____

Read through a few chapters from the book of Nehemiah. What are some threats that Nehemiah and his team faced, and how did they press beyond intimidating actions and words?

____

____

____

____

Have you asked God to give you favor in a situation and then pulled away when things started going your way? What made you apprehensive?

____

____

____

____

What negative thing or situation could be a sign that you are doing the right thing? Do you tend to view adversity as a sign that you are on the right track?

____

____

____

____

POWER PRAYER

Father, show me that Your promises are stronger than any enemy or adversary. Please reveal any traps set to discourage me or pull me away from your plan. Help me learn that the enemy of Your kingdom and my soul are the same. Most importantly, let me trust that You will never leave me or abandon me. You will safeguard my steps and protect my heart. Amen.

JOURNAL YOUR THOUGHTS

DIAMOND MOMENTS

You guide me with your counsel, and
afterward you will take me into glory
—*Psalm 73:24 (NIV)*

I was driving through Dallas, Texas, and noticed a billboard that advertised a well-known steak house in Houston. The sign encouraged those interested in dining at the five-star restaurant to take the next exit. I smiled and thought the billboard was slightly misleading because Houston is 240 miles south of Dallas. Obviously, the sign wasn't inferring Houston was around the corner. Rather, it was a reminder that the exit leading to Houston was a few feet ahead.

We don't need signs if we already know where we are going. We need signs if we are going somewhere new. When

I read through the Scriptures, I can't help but notice the number of brave men and women who relied on God to give them signs of confirmation. It wasn't that they were intimidated to do what God was asking them to do; they just wanted to ensure they were doing it at the right time or in the right way.

We need signs if we are going somewhere new.

Consider the account in Judges 6 where the military leader Gideon asked God for signs that He would give Israel victory. Gideon didn't ask for one sign but two distinct signs in twenty-four hours. A similar request was made by Abraham's servant when he went on a journey in search of a specific connection. Countless stories illustrate creative ways God gave signs to those who needed confirmation or reassurance.

Years ago, I hosted *The Diamond Leadership Conference*. Feeling uncertain about the logistics, budget, and size of the conference, I prayed and asked God to show me if I had made the right decision. On the way to meet with our conference staff the following day, I pulled into a convenience store. I noticed an object behind my left rear tire when I walked out of the store and back to the car. Thinking it might be a nail, I reached down to move it out of the way. The object wasn't a nail or a piece of glass but a large *diamond* ring. I can't explain the peace I felt when I placed that ring on my finger, and it fit perfectly. I left my number at the station, but no one claimed the ring. I felt the ring was a sign from God about the conference and wore it during the meetings. Today, I wear it often as a reminder that God is faithful to encourage us when we need it most.

WORDS OF COURAGE

It is easy to feel alone when we are walking through difficult situations. We must remember that during those hard times, God does not turn His children away but lovingly guides them through His plan of deliverance. If we are to live fearlessly, we must trust that God's purpose for our lives is exceedingly greater than our momentary rub with affliction. We must be brave enough to silence false emotions that stand between us and the victory God has planned.

REFLECTION QUESTIONS

Read Judges 6:33-40. Do you think Gideon asked God for double confirmation because he was concerned about the strength of Israel's army or because he was an insecure leader?

Are you comfortable asking God to confirm his plans through signs or other relatable methods?

____

____

____

____

What internal words of discouragement do you tend to speak over yourself—words that you are not good enough or not qualified enough? What hurt or wounds could be triggering those thoughts? Are you ready to shake free from negative thinking and move forward?

____

____

____

____

There is probably at least one dream in your heart that you have not fully committed to because of fear. Would a sign from God push you forward to go all in on your goals, or would you still hesitate? List the specific concerns that have prevented you from stepping out in faith. Now, list reasons those fears should look small compared to God's faithfulness. What is one small step you could take toward your dream?

____

____

POWER PRAYER

Father, I am confident You will show me how to walk through every test and trial. Thank You for sending words of encouragement and signs that point me in the right direction. I choose to rest in Your wisdom because You send the end of every situation.

JOURNAL YOUR THOUGHTS

SOMETHING GREATER

When I am surrounded by troubles,
you keep me safe. . . .
—Psalm 138:7 (GNT)

On New Year's Eve, I watched as a man was shot in the stomach. No, I wasn't attending a party, a sporting event, or walking in the city. The night of the shooting, I was sitting in church. My husband and I were at a watch night service and had just taken communion when I heard a loud noise and saw something sharp rip through the ceiling. The lights flickered, and ceiling tiles and other debris floated to the ground. At first, I thought the church had been hit by stray fireworks until the man sitting a few feet in front of me grabbed his midsection. Frightened, he jumped up and started screaming. He held his stomach and doubled over in pain. Expecting the worst, those of us around him looked for a place to take cover.

When the room finally calmed down, the man pulled his hand away from his stomach and lifted his shirt. Surprisingly, he didn't find blood but a bruise. Even though he had been shot by a .30-06 bullet, the bullet struck a thick metal button on his shirt and ricocheted to the ground. Things could have ended differently if the bullet had strayed a few inches to the left or right, especially considering that seated next to him was a young mother with a baby in her arms.

Sometimes, miracles can feel like near misses. I am sure that is what the sisters of Lazarus felt like after calling for Jesus and then burying their brother. In the natural, it appeared that they had missed the window for a miracle by minutes. It's probably safe to assume that the grave site conversation included a list of *what-if* scenarios:

What if they had sent word to Jesus sooner?

What if Lazarus had held on a few hours longer?

What if Jesus had come a few days earlier?

While everyone was questioning what could have happened or what should have been done, everything occurred just as it was predestined to occur. No, the miracle didn't happen when they expected it to or the way they imagined. And that was a good thing because God had scheduled something far greater than they could imagine—not a healing but a resurrection. Lazarus's name would go down in history not because a prayer was answered but because it was delayed.

I'm sure you have experienced what seems like narrow escapes in your faith journey as well. Take time to reflect on those events, and consider that sometimes, the best miracles are those that seem like near misses.

WORDS OF COURAGE

Even though it may not make sense at the time, sometimes God will delay answering prayer to give us a greater miracle. The important thing is not to lose faith while we are waiting. We should live in total confidence that God is writing an epic ending to our story. Even now, He is outlining chapters of our lives and waiting on us to come into agreement with His miraculous plans.

God may delay answering a prayer to give us a greater miracle.

REFLECTION QUESTIONS

Consider the man who was shot by a stray bullet. If you were he, how would you interpret what happened? Would you regret going to church that night or feel protected because you were in church?

____

____

Sometimes, moments can seem more tragic than they are. Think of something that happened to you that felt tragic at the time but, in reality, wasn't as bad as you had imagined. If something were to happen like that again, do you think you would react differently?

Imagine what it would have been like to be Lazarus—to be dead for three days and then called back to life. Imagine how often he was asked to share the same story and the pressure of trying to sound credible. Are there times when you hold back from sharing your account because you are afraid of what others will think about it? Do you think God expects us to share our testimonies?

Think of prayers that were answered but not in the way you imagined. What was your attitude like while you waited on the answer to arrive?

POWER PRAYER

Father, thank You for answering my prayer, even when the answer is different than what I imagined. I promise to trust You even when I don't understand Your timing. Please be patient with me as I learn to trust You in a new dimension. Amen.

JOURNAL YOUR THOUGHTS

A CHANCE TO DIE

"For whoever wants to save their life will lose it,
but whoever loses their life for me will save it."
—*Luke 9:24 (NIV)*

Most people are not willing to risk their lives for their profession. Maybe the disregard for her own life is what made Amy Carmichael an unsuspecting hero. Born in Ireland, Amy felt God wanted her to make a difference in the lives of people worldwide. Despite having caught neuralgia, a painful condition that would force her to spend weeks at a time in bed, she would follow the voice of God to Dohnavur, India. There she committed to learning the Tamil language so that she could communicate the gospel in the native language.[20]

20 Ian Hamilton, "Amy Carmichael (1867-1951): Missionary to India," *Radius International Pre-Field Church-Planting Training*, 18 Nov. 2018, https://www.radiusinternational.org/amy-carmichael-1867-1951-scottish-missionary-to-india/.

When she first arrived in India, she discovered horrors that were too dark for her mind to imagine. It was a local custom for young girls to be dedicated to the Hindu gods and then groomed to be sex slaves of the Brahmin priests. Since the girls were considered property of the gods,[21] they had no legislative rights and could be tortured without censure. As Amy encountered children with horrific tales of abuse, she was moved with compassion to establish a place where they could hide out and live protected. Under Amy's direction, Dohnavur became a sanctuary orphanage for the children of India. As word about the mission base spread, hundreds of hurting children came to the refuge. Her advocacy for human rights became a catalyst for social change.

Amy spent most of her life in great physical pain. Not only did she suffer from neuralgia, but later in life, she suffered a fall that resulted in her being bedridden for the last twenty years. Despite her infirmity, she kept the mission moving forward and wrote numerous books that helped abolish Hindu temple sex trafficking.

I wonder how different our lives would be if we loved others as Amy did. What if we lived from a position of pressing through our pain so we could heal the hurting around us? Being brave doesn't always mean making headline news, the cover of a tabloid, or having one's story go viral. Sometimes being fearless means leaving your country, fighting for a cause greater than your own, and suffering in silence.

---

21 Katherine Mayo, *Slaves of the Gods* (San Diego, CA: Harcourt, Brace, and Co., 1929) 123.

While serving in India, Amy received a letter from a young lady who was considering becoming a missionary. In the letter, she asked, 'What is missionary life like?' Carmichael wrote back, "Missionary life is simply a chance to die." That statement is the embodiment of the gospel message. May we push beyond the me-centric philosophies of our culture and learn to live and love fearlessly.

Push beyond the me-centric philosophies and learn to live and love fearlessly.

WORDS OF COURAGE

An article in a popular health and wellness magazine placed anxiety disorders at the top of the list of America's most common mental illnesses. Those living in today's society are not the first generation of people to find themselves on a quest searching for peace. Over two thousand years ago, the apostle Paul wrote to a group of believers at Philippi and gave them a prescriptive formula through which they could obtain and maintain a peaceful life. In his writings, he explained that one could cultivate peace by being prayerful, remaining thankful, and thinking about what is good. Perhaps we could add to that remedy the call to action to carve out time to serve those who are hurting.

REFLECTION QUESTIONS

If God asked you to make some sacrificial changes knowing that it would help others who were hurting, would you do what He asked? Amy left her country and family to work with strangers. Do you think that is asking too much of a person?

____

____

____

____

Amy was passionate about seeing children freed from the Brahmin priests. What humanitarian work are you passionate about? How do you support charities, social work, or non-profit organizations?

____

____

____

____

Sometimes serving others means that we have to set aside our suffering. Think of a time when you bypassed your heartache, so you could help someone else. Did you feel gratified by the sacrifice? Would you be willing to make the same kind of sacrifices on an ongoing basis? Take time to write out what living fearless means to you.

____

____

____

____

POWER PRAYER

Heavenly Father, empower me to reach beyond my pain and help others. Today, I commit to using my time, talents, and resources to bless others. Please multiply my efforts so that others can find help and peace.

JOURNAL YOUR THOUGHTS